Commendations

All human life-stories are special and distinctive, but some are so compelling that they ought to reach a wider audience. Such is Jen Kirby's story of struggle, anger, love and empowerment. In this honest and deeply-felt text, we are shown how a fight against systematic injustice can mould a life and a vocation, and how experience of the best and the worst of human nature can shape a Christian ministry across the world.

Diarmaid MacCulloch
Emeritus Professor of the History of the Church, University of Oxford
St Cross College and Campion Hall, Oxford June 2021

This book is the painful re-telling of what it was like to live under apartheid as a "coloured" person in love with a "white" man. Jenni Kirby relates the brutality of racism in South Africa, her involvement with the ANC and how that impacted her life with honesty and raw emotion. The reader is left knowing what it feels like to walk 'on shattered glass' as a woman of colour committed to justice and integrity for all. Jenni, in sharing her story, shows us how God's grace can penetrate the most difficult of circumstances and enable us to stand tall. This is a book that engrosses the reader and then shines a searing light on their need to take up the struggle for justice as well.

Sonia Hicks
President British Methodist Conference 2021/22

Although the title of this book, "Angry Love," is an oxymoron, it speaks about emotions and relationships, a must-read for those struggling with an understanding of the ambiguities in life, especially in contemporary post-apartheid South Africa.

The author's life is shaped by a quest for freedom at a very early age when her family was forcibly removed from their ancestral home by the apartheid regime's implementation of the notorious Group Areas Act of 1950. This left an indelible mark on her life and provided the metaphors, cultural touchstones and prism through which she viewed the world.

From the first chapter, Jenni Kirby takes the reader into her confidence and introduces one to her family circle, comrades and friends as she navigates her way through the cultural, social, and political terrain, where she grew up in an area designated for people classified as "coloured." She finds love across the racial divide, which ultimately resulted in her and her beau, Mark, seeking political asylum while she made her "home", exiled in Britain.

Despite her petite appearance and calm demeanour, Jenni is a courageous and transformative leader and lodestar for many who seek out genuine transformation in post-apartheid South Africa's society and faith communities. Her story is told with brutal honesty and integrity and is bound to strike chords of harmony or discord in the hearts of many. Her political activism together with a deep faith commitment led Jenni to seek a vocation in ministry. After the breakdown of her marriage and with emerging political changes in South Africa, Jenni found an opportunity to return to her "birth place" with her son, Themba, irresistible. Her homecoming, however, was bittersweet while adaptation and adjustment to "the new South Africa" presented several difficulties. Similar adjustment requirements in local South African churches proved unpalatable for Jenni. These circumstances promoted Jenni's return to Britain, where she says "she learnt to love again".

Angry Love is an epic tale of adversity, learning, and growth that nourished hope in the face of despair. Her story deserves to be heard by all who search for meaning, purpose, and a spirituality that empowers and equips the seeker for life's challenges in "transitional societies".

Readers will understand Jenni and a whole generation of black African activists better when they engage this narrative. I hope and trust that many, especially younger generations, will read "Angry Love". Above all, I trust they will draw inspiration from Jenni's story, trusting their instincts and following their hearts to work for justice and peace despite the obstacles that might stand in the way on the road of life. As Jenni testifies, there is nothing more rewarding.

This memoir is a treasure, written without pretence or rancour. Posterity will be richer for it.

Rev Ivan M Abrahams
General Secretary, World Methodist Council

Jenni Kirby

Memoirs of a Fellow
Seeker for a Better Country

Angry Love

Angry Love

Angry Love

© **Jenni Kirby**

Barnabas Publishers

19 Oude Pont Street

Wellington Business Park

Wellington

www.clf.co.za

Design and layout by: Joanne Bell

Cover design by: Joanne Bell

Printed and bound: Print on Demand (Pty) Ltd

First edition: 2021

ISBN: 978-1-86804-510-5 Angry Love

Angry Love

I dedicate this book

to my parents James and Clara Adams, who have taught their children to share our food, to pray when we're confused, and to live a meaningful life.

and

to my grandchildren Caleb Joel and Sadie Lila whom I love, and who are building a beautiful new world.

Contents

Foreword - Rev. Dr Lord Leslie Griffiths   XIII

Prologue   1

PART ONE: 'REMEMBER WHERE YOU COME FROM' 3

Chapter 1   A Black Dog   5

Chapter 2   The Shadow of Apartheid   11

    -    Families Divided   11

    -    Oppressed Community   15

    -    Love – 'Illegal and Immoral'   19

Chapter 3   Seeking Justice; glimpses of Grace 33

    -    Seeing things differently   33

    -    Building Community   35

    -    Conscientization   38

    -    What really matters   40

    -    The way of the cross?   42

    -    Imprisoned   50

    -    Moving on   52

Chapter 4   Leaving Home   55

PART TWO: NEW COUNTRY, NEW LIFE   **63**

Chapter 5   Alien and Accepted   **65**

       -    First Impressions   **65**

       -    New ways of seeing   **69**

       -    Reunion   **70**

       -    A wedding with a difference   **76**

       -    Transition   **81**

Chapter 6   Called to Serve   **83**

       -    Being in Community   **84**

       -    Learning and Growing   **85**

       -    Kingdom Lessons   **88**

       -    Living in two worlds   **91**

Chapter 7   Training and Transformation   **99**

       -    Another Party   **100**

       -    Kidnapped   **101**

       -    Celebration   **105**

Chapter 8   Ministry, for all   **109**

       -    Beginnings   **110**

       -    Reaching Out   **111**

       -    Pain and Loss   **113**

       -    On the move – again   **125**

PART THREE: SEEKING A BETTER COUNTRY **131**

Chapter 9 And Now? **133**

- A Place to stay **133**

- Work **134**

- Identity **136**

- A Flashback **138**

- New Ministry **140**

Chapter 10. Open to Grace **145**

- Open Doors **145**

- Open Hearts **149**

- Open Minds **154**

- Open Borders **155**

Chapter 11. Connecting **159**

- Connecting Families **159**

- Connecting Communities **160**

- Connecting Spirit and Action **164**

- Connecting Anger and Love **165**

Epilogue. Singing a new Song **169**

Foreword

"Angry love" is the perfect title for this book. Anger and love are the strong currents that swirl beneath the surface of its narrative. They flow, erupt, surge and envelop by turns. They're always there. The author is of diminutive stature and blessed, on first meeting, with a peaceful disposition. She's good to be with, hospitable, kind, open. But it doesn't take long to find the nerve ends which see her flare up in anger, or burst forth in love. Her anger stems from any injustice that crosses her field of attention while love is generated and released whenever she meets kindness or recognizes courage in a fellow human being. The combination of love and anger is formidable, a bit like wind and fire on the day of Pentecost. One of these elemental forces whips up the other and together they destroy or envelop all in their path. "Petite" she may be. But that in no way describes the punch she packs, the energy she stores, the passion she displays or the courage she shows when faced by human misery or powerlessness or marginalisation.

The story of her remarkable life sees her cast in a key role in two major moments of recent history. The first, of course, relates to her beginnings in South Africa, one of eleven children, with direct experience of the iniquitous policies of apartheid. Most people might claim some knowledge and might even rehearse a list of the major events of those years. The Group Areas Act, the Pass Laws, The Immorality Act and so many other punitive pieces of legislation underpinned the system of racial segregation. Then there were the massacres at Sharpeville and Soweto, the Rivonia trial that led to the imprisonment of the ANC high command, and the exile of activists. The struggle threw up so many larger-than-life personalities – people like Walter Sisulu, O. R. Tambo, Steve Biko, Desmond Tutu, Allan Boesak, Theo Kotze and, of course, Nelson Mandela. Who will forget the unbanning of the ANC or, supremely, the release of Nelson Mandela after an incarceration of 27 years, or the long lines of people queuing at the polling booths in 1994? This struggle caught the attention of the whole world. This was the big picture. And it was against this backdrop that ordinary people – men, women and children, black, white and coloured – lived their lives, took their chances, struggled to survive, hoped for a better day. It was a time when violence ruled the streets and the cruelty unleashed by the South African government and its agents is widely considered to have constituted a crime against humanity.

Our author was just one such South African citizen who lived through those critical years. Her story, a piece of micro-history in the making, needs to be told and heard along with others in order to earth our picture of the happenings of those years in the lives of ordinary people. The eviction of her family from their home in Constantia by agents of the apartheid regime is where her understanding began. Under the agency of the church and energised by her own personal faith, she found herself involved in community action of varying kinds but especially in the field of literacy. It also brought her up against the powers-that-be. The story she tells of her short stay in prison reveals both the horrors of the system and the astonishing interplay of character between her and the destitute women with whom she shared her cell.

Again and again, even in moments of despair, we hear mention of "Grace". The adjective "amazing" is never resorted to. It never needs to be. In one situation after another she seemed amazingly to find the good in all that's evil, light in the midst of darkness, hope where despair threatened to reign. Hers is a generosity of spirit which, while she ascribes it to God, is without any doubt part of her own character too.

When the opportunity arrives to further her studies in England, she describes her uprooting from the soil of her native land with rare poignancy. Who will fail to be moved by the message of her father as she departed for this new chapter in her life? "Remember you come from a great and proud people whose mouths are always wide with laughter and whose tears fall for every downtrodden soul... Walk tall. Walk proud. Take courage from those who paved the way for you to follow. God be with you 'til we meet again." This from a humble man, a driver, who'd never travelled anywhere in his life.

The story of Jennifer Sweet (Kirby) as an actor in the drama of South Africa's struggle for freedom simply has to be told. It takes the reader beyond newspaper headlines and beneath the views of pundits. It breathes and communicates on a person-to-person level.

If that were all, it would be plenty. But this book describes another drama and it's been her destiny to play her part in this too. This is the post-colonial drama of identity that's being played out in so many discussions of contemporary culture. The "settled" world of empire has disintegrated and is being reconfigured. There seem no fixed points. As the sleeve of an album by a rock band put it some years ago: "This is my truth, tell me yours." Each of us may tell our own story. And so, as the focus on individual human rights intensifies, answers are being sought to the oldest questions ever asked: Who am I? Where do I come from? Where am I headed? What are the values I should live by?

These questions have haunted our author since her birth. The colour of her skin, her gender, her faith defined the places where she could live and work as well as the role she could play. When she fell in love with a white man, she found herself the object of criticism from all sides – the government and its agents on the one hand and all her informal networks (including her family) on the other. And when, later, she travelled to England, she felt so much an alien cast among strangers. This drove her with passion into the work of exiled members of the ANC who were working for the overthrow of apartheid. She organised, addressed meetings, offered hospitality, gave her unstinted support to the cause. You might have thought this, above all, must have given her a clear sense of her identity. The sermon she preached at Saint Martin-in-the-Fields when Nelson Mandela was released from prison, so elegant and passionate, so celebratory and prophetic, reveals someone very comfortable in her own skin. And yet, for all that, other forces were eating away at her. She was finding her sense of self challenged as a real engagement with her new country developed.

She trained for (and was ordained into) the ministry of the Methodist Church in Britain. She served in a series of locations and was much appreciated by people, by white people as well as by those of other ethnic backgrounds. An old lady she lived with in Sheffield, total strangers addressing her fondly as "love," people from all walks of life, softened her feelings of otherness. She felt she was fitting into this new country of hers. She writes intriguingly on the question of "Identity" (see Chapter 9). But the painful breakdown of her marriage left her all at sea and she felt the need "to return home" (her own inverted commas) for solace and to get herself together again. She believed she could take up the life she'd lived there before her departure for England. And yet, as she reports so candidly, that just couldn't be done. "I missed the familiarity of London," she writes before adding a word about missing (of all things) "the cold winter mornings." She was clearly all over the place. So much so that, within a very short time, despite herself, she found herself heading back to England.

Her rootlessness at this time is the experience of so many

just now. She didn't seem to belong anywhere any more. She knew the vulnerability of the migrant – again a word current in contemporary debates about the plight of so many people in the world we've created for ourselves.

Jennifer is so transparent about the two loves of her life, Mark and Ermal. Her testimonies to each of them are beautiful, laced with love and admiration alike. The breakdown of her relationship with Mark is described with tragic intensity. She writes of the relationship with Ermal with deep affection. Her first love came about in defiance of the law of the land and could only be developed by leaving South Africa. The second was with a black man whose culture and antecedents hailed from the Caribbean. So many strands are woven into the whole. It has all been so risky. Much was built. A great deal was broken.

She relates how, on one occasion, after sharing something of her story, a member of her audience gave her some wise advice: "You must learn how to walk on the broken pieces". And so she did. And so she does. "I am a different person from the young woman who set foot on these shores almost forty years ago," she writes.

After six spells living alternately in two countries, after wondering how best to integrate her longings, loves, hopes and memories, she has arrived at a point where she can reflect with gratitude on a life full of incident and, faced with those primordial questions about human existence, she can conclude: "What we have learned is that we don't have to live with a continuing feeling of 'not belonging' or of home being somewhere else; we have the privilege of belonging fully in (at least) two different places at the same time, England and South Africa; we are not bound by borders, and can relish the richness and diversity of being Kingdom people, people open to being transformed by Grace."

What a life! What a story! Now read on.

Rev Dr Lord Leslie Griffiths

Angry Love

Prologue

The kitchen fell silent, suddenly; and, as one, the five women who had been chatting away as we tidied up following yet another church function, turned in my direction, all with widened eyes, two with mouths fallen open. I had just mentioned casually that I could still remember how to make a Molotov Cocktail. (Well, you know how one thing leads to another when women get talking!)

This was not what they expected to hear from their minister. They knew that I had 'a past'; that I had been part of the political struggles in South Africa, but incendiary devices were something else. So, I told them part of my story – how a model young Christian woman became a militant activist, serving in organisations that worked for the liberation of South Africa.

When I stopped speaking, their only question was, "Will you teach us how to make Molotovs?" I didn't, as I immediately thought that this was not something that devout members of a respectable church in Walthamstow, London, needed for their continuing development; but they did make me think further about how I had changed, and wonder about when it had begun and what had motivated me.

John Bell of the Iona Community writes of being "Inspired by love and anger": was that how it was for me? Love and anger have been so interwoven in my life, sometimes it's hard to know where each begins or ends.

A long time ago, a theologian friend, Elsa Tamez from Mexico, told me that "only a suffering God is of any use". And then an incident took place which made me think long and hard about this statement; an incident that made me question this 'suffering of God' in human life. It was an unexpected, brutal, traumatising event, involving the suffering of an innocent child, and I found myself swearing at God. Even as I did so, I asked myself how could I, a committed Christian, swear at the Almighty God?! But I did. It was a guttural utterance that came from deep within; I swore loudly at God out of my anger and pain, feeling the pain of a mother who mourns for her murdered child.

But let me go back to the beginning.

Angry Love

PART ONE

'REMEMBER WHERE YOU COME FROM'

Angry Love

Chapter 1
A Black dog

I was a premature baby and my first 'cot' was a size seven shoe-box. The doctor told my mother that I would not live to see my first birthday. My lungs were so under developed, I could not breathe properly; I suffered from 'a weak chest' and other ailments, and my parents could not afford the necessary medical treatment, so they resorted to the skills and the traditional medicines and herbs that had been passed down from one generation to the next in the Coloured community. Both my maternal and paternal grandmothers cared for me as they wrapped me in red flannel, and massaged me with traditional oils as they prayed over me. The Methodist minister was called in to say prayers, the church community was praying; my parents spent time on their knees beseeching God to spare the life of their first born – and I survived.

I grew up on a farm called Silversands in Constantia, Western Cape, a beautiful place with sprawling acres of grape vines and oak trees, cypress trees and jacarandas. We lived in a row of cottages where all the other farm workers and their families lived. Our road was called Strawberry Lane. I can't remember now if there were any strawberries around ... there must've been, I guess. I only remember the rows and rows of luscious grapes.

I remember the many sunny days, while the grownups were picking grapes and putting them in huge baskets on a tractor, we the children were lying on our backs, slithering underneath the vines, stuffing ourselves with the sweetest, most juicy grapes on earth. I remember how full I felt when I went home with my dress streaked with red from the grape juice and the taste of grapes in my mouth would linger for hours and hours afterwards.

It was an idyllic childhood. We had a home, we had fresh food every day. My Dad had a little vegetable patch in the back growing beans, carrots, cabbages and mealies (sweetcorn). In the front garden he grew baby roses and sweetpeas. We also had lots of chickens. The farm produced and sold poultry and wine.

There were six of us at the time: myself, four sisters and baby brother, Mervin. Our days were spent running around the farm. Sometimes we would run up to the big white, thatch roofed farm house with black gables and the two family dogs would run us over and lick our faces. They would get so excited when they saw us, they would pant and give short, happy snorting-barking yelps. Sometimes the 'madam' would come out and call us into the kitchen where the cook was instructed to give us ginger beer and whatever left-overs was around from the day before (usually a sweet syrupy twisted doughnut or *vetkoek*). The cook was a relative of my mothers' and she'd been working for Miss Shelly a long time.

At the age of five or six, I wasn't aware of apartheid, or that we were oppressed in any way. I just accepted things as they were, like most children would, I guess. My parents were kind and loving and took care of us; we were surrounded by relatives and friends who all worked on the farm doing different jobs.

My father was the driver and he drove a truck with the name of the farm painted on the side: Silversands Poultry Produce. He was also the assistant 'manager'. This meant that every Friday he would sit on an upturned wooden box next to '*Meneer* Kleynhans', the white manager, and hand over the workers' wages as Mr. Kleynhans read out each name from the long brown book he had on the table in front of him. I think they might also have been given a bottle of wine, I'm not sure, but I do remember on Fridays there was a different atmosphere around and in the evenings most of the workers, wives and children would gather round and there would be loud music, dancing, much laughter and the men played dominoes on an old farm house table outside in the yard. It was such a jolly atmosphere and my Mother would produce one of her *melkterte* – a creamy custard on a shortcrust pastry base, with grated nutmeg on top – she made the best *melktert* for miles around. You can be sure at every birth, death, or wedding my mother's *melktert* took centre place on the table!

Constantia was, and still is, a beautiful place to live. There were trees of all kinds lining the roads and everything was always green, summer and winter. It was a quiet place, only the white people had cars and they never roared down the road, always driving slowly and waving to us when they come into or went out of the farm. We were surrounded by huge mansions and many of them had 'servants quarters' built at the back where the domestic worker-cum-cook and the gardeners lived during the week. At the weekends they would go off to visit their families.

Angry Love

Only the farm workers like my Dad, uncles and aunts (they weren't really my uncles and aunts, but it was the custom to address every grown-up as uncle and aunt) and their families lived permanently on the farm. We were like one huge happy family and our childhood was spent running carefree among the vines, climbing trees, chasing chickens, helping our mother around the house and pushing baby brother Mervin in an old rickety push chair which first belonged to the white babies in the big house, but was given to us when they left for boarding school and the 'madam' was clearing out all their stuff. I can't remember the children's names anymore, but they were very young when they were packed off to school in England. We were given all their cast offs, clothes, toys and once, a push chair with one wheel missing.

* * *

One day my Dad came home, greeted my Mum with his usual kiss on the cheek and said rather gruffly: "Claire, come to the room, please". They disappeared into their bedroom and we could hear their voices rising and falling and my Dad sounded as if he had a cold, or ... he was crying! My mother was definitely crying because we could hear her saying over and over again in between sobs: "What are we going to do? Oh Lord, what are we going to do? Where must we go-ooo?" The last word ended in a shriek.

I remember waking up one night and heard a noise outside our window. When I looked out, I saw my Dad kneeling in the sand. I couldn't make out the words he uttered, but he was weeping. Sometimes he would look up to the dark sky, sometimes he would just put his head down on his arms, his shoulders heaving. I felt a knot in my throat, I didn't know what to do. I felt so helpless and upset. My Dad loved this farm, he was born here and knew no other life – nor did he have any skills – having left school at 15 he could read and write but driving was what he could do and he was a damn good driver! Not only did he drive the large farm truck, he also drove the owner in his Mercedes around, to and from the airport.

Now we have to leave this place all because we have a government who look after those with a white skin (and money), and they must have the best this land of ours has to offer. Constantia was going to be declared a "Whites Only" designated area. That day the farm manager called all the workers together and told them we have to pack up our home and leave the farm by the end of the following month.

We were not allowed to live in Strawberry Lane anymore.

If we do decide to remain, we would be forcibly removed by the police, who had the legal right to chase out of this area anyone who is not white. Mr Kleynhans said the Big Boss, the owner of the farm, would allow us to remain an extra 14 days to give Dada time to find us a place to live.

How or what my dear father did I don't know, but within six weeks he found us a house in a suburb called Heathfield. It was a small semi-detached house in a paved street and friendly neighbours on either side. We soon became firm life-long friends with the Arendse, Erasmus and Van Diemen families.

My mother was pregnant when we moved from Constantia, and within our first year in the new house, she gave birth to my brother Jakes. Jimmy, Jerry, Edmund and two more sisters, Priscilla and Patti were all born in Heathfield.

We had a house full of children, a large back garden where my Dad continued to grow vegetables for the pot; we had chickens and an Alsatian dog named Flash. Whereas on the farm we saw and spoke to white people almost every day, in this area there were no whites, only Coloured families.

There was a railway line dividing us from the Whites who lived in the leafy suburb of Bergvliet. Heathfield was quite a middle class Coloured suburb and most of our neighbours were either in the teaching profession, social workers or in Administration or Finance in the City of Cape Town.

* * *

The reality of Apartheid had begun to affect me, and it was not long before I felt its impact in further ways. The first might seem a trivial incident, but its effect has been lasting.

I was ten years old, and my father and I were walking past the park in Newlands. "Dada, why can't we go in? Come on, come push me high up on the swing!" I ran and dragged my father behind me towards the open gate. He pulled back, "No, Jenni; no *bokkie* (sweetheart) it's not for us. This park is for white people only. We are not allowed in there!"

I stood holding on to the railings. Watching the little white children on the swings and seeing them go up and down the slide. Laughing, running around and enjoying themselves as only children can. Black nannies were sitting on the grass keeping a watchful eye over their white charges. They, too, were not allowed (legally) to sit on the beautiful wooden benches in the park either! Each green bench had a large sign written on it, "For Whites only". I watched, my heart longing to go in and play.

Angry Love

Then something caught my eye. A dog, a big black dog ran across the grass, lifted up his leg and peed all over the bench that said "For Whites only". I laughed out loud. My father grabbed my hand and still laughing we walked on. I couldn't wait to get home and tell my sisters and brothers about the black dog who didn't know he was *not* allowed to pee on the bench marked "For Whites only".

* * *

Home was a comforting place to be. It was noisy with 5 sisters and 5 brothers, a dog, a cat, and chickens who didn't know their place – they were forever in the house under chairs or behind the couch. We also had my grandma living with us after my maternal grandpa died. Ours was the noisiest house in the street. Always bustling and bursting with the neighbours' children gathered on our stoep, or kicking a ball in the backyard with my bothers.

Home was the place waiting for me when I returned from youth camps – or after a great night out with friends – and always grandma was there, ever ready with a hot cup of cocoa and to chat about the evening's jollifications. Grandma was always so interested in our young lives and loves and her ear was a ready 'confessional' for lamenting a broken friendship, or to rave about the attractive qualities of a boy I admired. What I

Sunday school – on the photo I have been marked with a *

remembered most was her wearing her trademark apron with the large front pocket; this was the carrier for the eggs we collected from the hens in the yard, but it had mysterious inner chambers, because from it could come at a moment's notice a hankie to wipe a snotty nose; and no time later, a delightful toffee – all very unhygienic by today's standards, but a source of wonder and comfort for a child then.

Neighbours, family and friends gathered regularly for an impromptu braai. Family and relatives dropped in without prior notice and they come laden with platters of meat, or cakes to share. And the women would be there in the kitchen, gossiping and cooking more food.

Home was laughter, singing and dancing round the kitchen table! Home was my grandma saturating the house with the smell of bread baking in the oven, and her brown coffee pot bubbling on the stove that seemed to be perpetually crackling with a burning fire!

In the evenings my father and grandmother would entertain us with stories from the 'olden days', and my mother forced us to read and recite by heart, all the Psalms of David. I grew up in a happy home and had a deep sense of family and belonging which gave me stability in the turbulent years that were to come.

Chapter 2

The Shadow of Apartheid

Apartheid was like an ominous, poisonous shadow that blighted the lives of Black and Coloured people throughout South Africa, and I came to see, more and more, both how stupid it was and how harmful it could be. My family is a microcosm of how subtle divide and rule played out in our lives and how we absorbed it as the norm.

Families Divided

Like many 'Coloured' families, ours was of mixed heritage. My paternal grandmother's family came from St. Helena and she married my grandfather whose descendants came from somewhere in India. My mother's grandmother was from Khoi descent, and Mothers' grandfather was a Boer, of Afrikaner descent. My mother had light skin, green eyes and 'in-between' hair, as they say in the Cape. Both my mother and her sister were classified as "other Coloured". They fell between the cracks; they did not look white enough to be classified as "white" and they do not look Coloured enough to be classified as "Coloured". This is the blurred edges of the colour pendulum. My mother's sister, auntie Phillida, who inherited a beautiful peaches and cream skin, blue eyes, and light brown hair (which she dyed light brown and straightened with 'Wella Straight') married a white man, who was a pilot in the Canadian air force. They lived in Bergvliet, a suburb in Cape Town, which in the 60's and until 1994 was exclusively white. I remember visiting her with my Mother. We had to go round by the side gate, which had a sign that said: "Blacks and hawkers' entrance". Imagine it: she was my mother's only sister and we, her family, had to go round the back! We were not allowed to come through her front door in case one of her white neighbours saw us Coloureds walking through the front door! My aunt, Phillida, was ashamed of her own family and of where she came from!

After living her life as a "play white" for several years, she and her husband emigrated to Canada where my aunt gave birth to a child. This little girl came out a little bit too brown to be white, so my aunt sent her home to grow up with my grandma; her name was Clarissa. She grew up with hatred for her own mother, for rejecting her because she wasn't white enough. Auntie Clarissa never went to visit her mother or saw her other siblings (who, it seems, turned out 'nice and white'). She married a man of Xhosa descent, out of love or revenge I don't know, but now we have cousins who are light skinned, and we have cousins who are dark skinned. We all grew up together as a family. I mention these things because it describes the type of philosophy that 'appears' to be at work among the community of that area, which puts us against each other so very often, not only in our community, but also in the church. One of the tools of apartheid's divide and rule strategy was to use those of light skin against the dark skin – our different hues were used to create distrust and envy.

As children we accepted things as we find them, but I knew life was better if you are white skinned – you can get away with a lot of things. In those days, if you were a light skinned Coloured girl, you got the 'front jobs' – like a receptionist in the hotel, or a switchboard operator in a block of offices, or a sales girl in a posh shop like Stuttafords. Many of those Coloured girls played white. I don't blame them. Life was made easier for them. What I only realised much later was that in a 'divide and rule' scenario, the third party is the only one that benefits. Never the two sides opposed to each other.

One of my aunt's daughters, Patsy, was so light skinned, with blue eyes and fine straight hair, she could be mistaken for a white girl. Whenever we have to take the train somewhere, we would send Patsy to the other ticket office, the side that said "Whites Only" to buy our train tickets. We would stand on the platform, as nonchalantly as we can chatting away while waiting for Patsy to come from the white side with all our tickets! I remember how gleeful we were and how superior we felt in front of the astonished queue of Coloureds waiting patiently to be served by the same clerk who also serves the 'other side'. Of course, if there's a white person waiting on the 'white side', he would serve them first and thus quite a number of passengers would miss their train.

I couldn't articulate it at the time, and I wasn't aware of racism in the family, but I do remember the prejudiced 'off the cuff' remarks my mother would make, especially when she took us girls shopping for clothes, or when busy sewing our dresses for Christmas. I remember her saying to one of the aunts: "I found this lovely blue material that I can make dresses with for the girls. But Jennifer, *ai hene*, I don't know, she is so *blou* (so dark), this colour won't suit her". Or, the aunties, when they talk about us would refer to me, not by name, but as the 'dark one', saying, for example: "Oh, you're talking about the *dark* one, *ja* she's the clever one". These remarks, innocently said as a joke, left me with the impression there's something wrong with me. That I wasn't nice, not attractive. Sometimes one of the aunties would call out to me, "Come here, *kaffir meid*, let me plait your hair".

I had long beautiful shiny black hair which my grandma Annie said I inherited from her, from her Island foremothers, as she referred to them. She was my paternal grandmother and she was born in St. Helena. When she married my grandfather, who was born in Durban (a marriage between a Botswana woman and an Indian man), moved to Constantia in Cape Town, where my father was born.

I met my paternal grandfather properly for the first time when I was about nine years old. I guess he must've been around at family gatherings before then, because I vaguely recollect a shadowy figure lifting me up and hugging me. But I didn't really know him because my grandfather on my father's side was classified as 'Indian' under the Group Areas Act. At that time and for a short period he lived somewhere else.

On one occasion when he came to visit us, I went with my grandmother to the bus stop to see him off. A police van with two white officers drove up and the policemen demanded to know what he was doing in that area. Pappa pointed to my grandma, and said that he was visiting his wife. One of the officers laughed sneeringly and told Pappa to run. The officers then drove behind him, shouting, "Run, *coolie*, run". It's still painful to recall the sight of my lovely grandpa disappearing down the road, running like a hunted animal, not looking back, as he was chased by two white youngsters in a police van.

Domestic service, working as maids and cleaners, is often seen as something that black women did at that time, but Coloured women also did these jobs, and in addition to the full-time demands of caring for her own family, my mother worked part-time as a cleaner. I remember one day my mother was ill and couldn't get to work. When I came home from school, she asked me to go with her to the house where she worked, so that she could do what had to be done before 'the madam' came home. The house was in a mess. The kitchen sink was full of dirty dishes. In the bedroom, there were dirty panties lying on the floor, alongside a pair of underpants, and clothes strewn over the chair and on the bed.

My mother told me to pick up all the dirty clothes and put them into the laundry basket in the bathroom, and to hang up the clean ones in the wardrobe. "*Haai*, Mummy, can't she put her own dirty panties in the laundry basket? Must you pick these up every day?" "*Ai* Jennifer, my child," she replied, "Stop your questions. These white people just do what they want. I suppose 'cause they white' they can do it. We need her money. Your Dada works very hard, but there's too many mouths to feed and too many bodies to clothe, I have to do this extra work so that I can buy your school clothes."

I felt ashamed that my mother had to go and pick up another woman's dirty knickers so that she could have enough money to buy my school shirts. I was angry at this white woman. Did she not know that my Mother was a teacher before she married my father? Did she not know that my mother influenced young minds and shaped their thought processes? I felt a deep sense of revulsion. But I also wanted to know why and how this all came to be, and why God didn't do something about it. If we are all equal in God's sight, why this? These were questions that would trouble me for a long time to come, and over the years more questions were added, and only slowly did some answers emerge.

Recognising the sacrifices my parents were making, I worked even harder at school and completed Matric. After I left school and began working in a clerical post, I was able to begin contributing to the family finances. Each week I would hand my unopened pay packet over to my Mum. What has stayed in my mind to this day was my mother kneeling at the side of the bed with my wage packet opened in front of her, asking God to bless the money I've earned. Afterwards, first thing she did was to put my 'tenth' in the church envelope, then she gave me what she thought was enough for my personal use. Up to this day, whenever I was paid my stipend, I do what my Mother did. Give thanks and ask God to bless his money that He made possible for me to have.

* * *

Shortly before my nineteenth birthday, I walked into the post office with my granddad to pick up his pension. In those days you were given a post office book with which to draw and deposit money. (Coloureds and Blacks were not allowed to open a bank account then; only Whites were allowed a bank account in a proper bank). We walked into the post office. My grandfather was a tall man with beautiful snow-white hair and leather brown skin. He always walked upright, his back straight; he looked magnificent, like a warrior.

Anyway, on this day I went with him because he promised me a new pair of shoes for my nineteenth birthday. We got to the counter and the young white man pushed a piece of paper towards my granddad. "Sign here," he said. My grandpa said, "I can't write, *my baas*." This young *snotkop* then said: "Then make a cross here, you *aap*" (you monkey). My grandpa, with his head bent low, did what was asked and his pension money was pushed across the counter.

We walked out of the post office, but something was different. Whereas before he had walked in tall and proud, holding my hand. Now, leaving the post office, my grandpa looked smaller, shrunken into himself, bent over, and he didn't hold my hand; he wouldn't even look at me! I looked up at his face. Up to this day I cannot describe the emotions I saw in his face: anger, rage, humiliation, sadness, frustration – and defeat.

It was then I made a vow to myself: I vowed that never, never, would I witness another human being having to endure treatment like this just because they are black, or because they cannot write or read.

The year when I turned twenty, I trained to become a Literacy Teacher and I taught many people to read and write.

Oppressed Communities

In the meantime, I lived a sort of 'double life': in one world, as the eldest sibling, I would watch over my brothers and sisters at home, taking responsibility from an early age, and as a model young Christian woman, I would attend church every Sunday, teach in the Sunday School, sing in the church choir, and for good measure served as the Circuit Youth Worker, covering the six churches in our Circuit; and in my other world, I was becoming increasingly active in passive resistance activities – discovering more about my own history, becoming more conscious of the injustices of the present regime, and learning strategies for resisting and overcoming its evil.

I remember going to visit my aunt who was a domestic worker for a rich white family in Sea Point. I waited, with others, for the bus, and when it came, we had to go upstairs to sit; downstairs was for Whites only. An elderly lady with shopping bags and trailing leg, struggled up the stairs. I grabbed one of her bags. She trudged up step by step - keeping the bus waiting (there was a long queue of Coloured peoples behind her). When we finally got upstairs all the seats were taken. She just went and sat on the floor and everyone who wanted to get off the bus, had to climb over her and her bags!

Something came to sit on my chest - mixed emotions of fear, anger and frustration - especially when I looked around as I got off the bus and saw the few white people seated, and all the rest of the empty seats downstairs which could've been made available for us to sit in.

It was about that time that I enrolled on a Training Course for Literacy Teachers that was run by Catholic Sisters in Hanover Park, Cape Town, even though the regime did not approve of its contents. I then volunteered to deepen my experience by going to Botswana to be trained in Paolo Freire's methodology, which was designed to create critical consciousness in the minds of students.

* * *

So, from the age of twenty, I began teaching people to read and write. We had many women working in the clothing industry who couldn't read - some could read haltingly, and others couldn't write. It was after one of my Literacy Sessions, on my way home, I was standing at the bus stop. Already there were two black women standing there waiting for the bus, one a domestic worker (judging from her blue overalls and white apron). We greeted one another and then just stood and waited. You could wait for hours for a bus to come trundling along the Sea Point upper Main Road in those days.

A police van came cruising along the road. One policeman jumped out and begin to demand the women show him their *dompas* (ID document which every black person was forced to carry, to prove they can live in the country of their birth). One of the ladies started to cry as she rummaged in her bag. I was quite annoyed with her. "Ag Mama, don't cry in front of them! Don't show them you're afraid". She responded in Xhosa, "Can you speak Afrikaans?" she asked me. "Tell the *baas* that I have a pass. But I have forgotten to put it in my bag when I left home in a hurry. I just came out to buy nappies for my baby. I ran out of nappies. I left her with my neighbour; she is only nine months old."

As she speaks, tears are streaming down her face. I told the white policeman that this lady is breast feeding and needed

Angry Love

to get home to her small baby. He looked at me and told me to shut up "You blerrie *hotnot*. You think you clever, *nê*!" He went and stood in front of the woman, ripped open her blouse. He put his hand into her bra and squeezed her breast! The milk squirted out and made a half moon loop across his chin. She screamed! I screamed. The other lady screamed and tried to pull him off this mother. He laughed, sneered at us and pushed her into the back of the police van.

Crying I ran to the phone box which I noticed on the street corner, so that I could phone the Black Sash Office. Of course, when I got to the public phone box, all the wires were pulled out of the wall – there was no way I could contact anyone! We didn't have mobile phones in the 1970s. My heart was heavy as I made my way back to the bus stop. The bus had come and gone. I was by myself. Just weeping. The two ladies are gone – one to her home, or the employers house, the other on her way to a police cell. All because she didn't have her pass with her!

Oh, dear Lord, I prayed, what is going on in this beautiful land? What will happen to her baby now? Who is going to look after the little one? What will her neighbour do now that she's not going to turn up? Why this? How can that police man do what he just did! I suppose he can, he's white. He's a police man. He has every apartheid legislation behind him and the power of the State to support him. She is nothing to him! She is only a black person. A woman whose husband is somewhere working on the mines. A black mother with no legal rights, or resources. A mother who came to do what thousands of mothers do every day: to buy nappies for their babies. Now she is locked up in a cell. Alone. With a bag of nappies. And her tears. Where does she live? Oh, dear Lord, what can I do?

* * *

Love and anger burned in me, and I knew that I had to do more.

* * *

Fortunately, the church recognised my passion and tried to make sure that it was used to good effect. I was offered training so that I could become involved in different aspects of social care and community development. I was able to take part in a National Youth Leadership Training Programme that brought together fifteen participants from all over Southern Africa, reflecting the 'rainbow nation', long before that phrase was coined. Black, white, and brown people were all thrown together for three months of intensive training, which would then be followed by a year on attachment to a local church community. It was called "Give a year of your life to God".

This training complex named Koinonia, nestled at the foot of the Valley of a Thousand Hills in Durban, far removed from the turmoil in the streets of Soweto where many young students lost their lives that year, 1976. But we did visit many of the homes in the aftermath of the Soweto riots and we also attended several funerals. One of these I will never forget.

A group of us went out to the town to attend this funeral because one of the participants on the Course was a neighbour to the family. We were told that two children from one family had been taking part in a demonstration, and that one, a boy, was shot in the heart and died in the street; his sister, aged eleven, was also shot and was taken to the nearest hospital, where she was not admitted. The friends had rushed to the next hospital, but by the time she was on the operating table, the little girl had lost so much blood, she died.

On the day of their funeral, the papers reported an attendance of 3000 people. At the graveside, I was standing close to the mother whose face was contorted with grief as the tears just kept on rolling down her cheeks; it was as if her whole face was crying. A young woman standing next to me burst out screaming: "I hate the police. When will they stop shooting innocent children? I wish someone would come and shoot them!"

The Mother, turned to her and said: "No, my dear, we must not hate the police. They, too, are children from a mother's womb. My children have died. I will never see them again. But they have not died in vain, they have died so that one day, other children may live in freedom in the land of their birth."

I could not believe what I was hearing! This mother had just buried two of her children; children who did not die from a childhood illness but were calculatedly murdered: killed because they happened to be black in white South Africa!

Never before or since have I met anyone who so perfectly demonstrated *grace* for me as this mother did: her words were spoken so clearly, so calmly; there was power in those words of grace, defying every human instinct for revenge, and they shaped the course of my discipleship forever. And in the dark periods to come in my own life, I summoned up hope and strength and perseverance, all because on that day I saw a reflection of God's grace in the life of an ordinary, courageous woman. An unknown woman taught me how to walk on shattered glass.

Love – 'Illegal and Immoral'

But the shadow of Apartheid that affected me most deeply was the one that it cast over my closest personal relationship: I dared to fall in love with someone whose colour was different from mine, and that, in the eyes of the apartheid regime, was not only illegal, it was immoral – and that has had an impact on all the rest of my life.

I close my eyes and I can see Mark, the young man who had opened my heart's door wide, and awakened within me a deep love for him. Even though it was a love that had all the odds stacked against it: there we were, a young Coloured woman and a young white man, living in two separate worlds in apartheid South Africa. We found so much energy and support and growth and happiness in and with each other, that we were (or thought we were) prepared to overcome all the racial, political and social obstacles that we encountered in a segregated society during those early years. And in some ways, it was those very circumstances that fuelled our growing relationship. Strangely enough, again it was the church that enabled this coming together of our two worlds. All through the years of racial divide, the Methodist Church's policy was emphatic in its support for non-racial and innovative learning initiatives.

I met Mark on a three-month Community Development Training Programme initiated by the Methodist Church, under the umbrella of the Churches Urban Planning Commission. At that time, I was assisting Social Workers in one of the most deprived and poverty-stricken areas in the Western Cape. I eagerly welcomed this opportunity to gain some formal qualification so that I could make my dream come true, which was to help the people among whom I lived to better themselves and to build a strong and viable community. My passion was to empower those women who do the most menial of jobs, the tired women I know who sweep and wash and scrub for others.

So, when this Course was advertised in the church bulletin, I applied and was accepted. My friend Vivian who also enrolled for this Course, offered me a lift in her car. The course was being held in Muizenberg, which was a short drive from where we lived, and we arrived at the Training Centre well ahead of time, but someone else was there before us. Sitting outside on the porch of the building was a young white man with a backpack thrown carelessly on the ground next to him. He wore a light green jacket, white Indian cotton shirt, an old pair of blue jeans with holes in them and a navy spotted bandana round his neck. The sun was shining and it painted his long blond hair into a burnished orange and gold colour: he was beautiful! He wore big tear drop spectacles and when Vivian invited him to sit with us in the car, he unfolded himself off the stoep and slowly sauntered over and introduced himself.

I noticed his very blue eyes, soft and gentle eyes they were. "Mark", he said with a beaming smile, and stuck out his hand. His grip was firm and his hands cool to the touch. "Hey, I'm Vivian and this is my friend, Jenni," replied Vivian. As we sat in the car, waiting for someone to unlock and let us in, we chatted and shared pleasantries as one does when you're strangers thrown together by circumstance. I stole discreet glances trying to figure out what this young man's motive was for enrolling on this church-based community development training programme. He didn't look the usual churchy type and his dress code was wacky and hippy! I was fascinated, curious and drawn to him simultaneously.

Here we are in a very un-South African situation, and yet this guy was so relaxed in our company and so at ease with himself. Sitting cosily in a car chatting to two Coloured women – as if we are friends, and this was the most natural thing to do! For goodness's sake, it is 1978 – in apartheid South Africa! As far as I know, white people are rich. White people buy expensive clothes, they don't wear jeans with holes in them. The white people I knew would not dream of speaking to people like me as if we are friends! What's up with him? Is there something wrong with him; does he know there is Apartheid? I thought, maybe he's from overseas? I hear that overseas they don't have Apartheid and everyone mixes with everyone else.

Our first evening whizzed past; I have hazy recollections of an overview about the Course, and introductions all-round the group of twenty participants. Next, we were given ground rules for the six weeks of communal living in the Training Centre, which would also involve some working in the community. This was the first Community Development Training of its kind to be introduced in the whole of Southern Africa: and we were the pioneers. Des Adendorff, the Programme Director, informed us that on certain days we will be joined by lecturers from the Sociology Department of the University of Cape Town, and that professionals like lawyers, social workers, nurses and doctors working in the Community will come and share their experiences of working among the people living on the Cape Flats.

Just before the session ended on that first night, we played a game – an ice breaker – called 'pass the parcel' sitting in a circle. In this instance a huge blue plastic beach ball was passed from hand to hand while lively music was blasting from the record player. Each time the music stopped, the person holding the ball has to answer a question, for example: where do you come from? Why did you come on this Course? It was fun and highly revealing.

There were six white people in the group, including Mark and someone called André – a young guy from France, who was living with his grandparents for a year, gap year, I think he said. Afterwards we, the Coloureds and Blacks, as we were classified in those days, asked him what a gap year was. He said he wanted to travel before going to university and that he was interested in the 'other' Communities living in the Western Cape. On that Training Programme in 1978, as in the course I attended in Durban in 1976, we again represented the "rainbow people" of South Africa.

What I remember vividly was how quiet and laid-back Mark was in comparison to the other white males on the Course. Most of the men had something to say about everything, but they were friendly, not arrogant. The women hardly spoke on that first evening. Mark was sitting opposite me in the circle, and from time to time I caught him staring at me, of course I was sneaking quick looks at him too!

By the end of the evening most of us were still in a convivial mood and wanted to continue the animated conversations that erupted since the beginning of the opening session. We were all very conscious that this ethnically mixed gathering was a rarity in apartheid society. As I watched from my vantage corner on a comfortable couch, I observed the different dynamics in the small groups dotted round the large room. It seemed the white participants were doing much of the talking, others were a bit more cautious, cordial and reserved. I understood completely. I, personally, wouldn't immediately upon meeting, talk to any white South African. I wouldn't know what their motives were; and why should I talk to them here and now in this place when I know tomorrow they will pass me in the street as if I don't exist?

So, I watched and absorbed and wondered. There were three people chatting around the coffee machine in the corner of the room, Mark among them. He turned away from the trio and made his way across the room to the couch where I was sitting in conversation with Sister Mary-Anthony, a nun from Northern Ireland, who was now living and working among the people in Manenberg, a township in Cape Town.

"Would you ladies like a hot chocolate before bed-time?" It

was Mark; he was smiling broadly and his eyes held a great kindness in them. I don't really like hot chocolate, but since he held out two cups, I said yes thank you, and took one of the paper cups from him. "Get one for yourself and come sit here with us" invited Sister Mary-Anthony. He came and sat with us and we chatted. He was interesting to listen to, delicious to look at and he knew a great deal about the situation in our country.

We talked about our families, our land, the turmoil and unrest since the 1976 riots in Soweto. He was well informed and he spoke with passion and compassion about how the inequalities in our society is built on the exploitation of Blacks by Whites, how the stable economy is produced by cheap black labour. He said that he believed that we should all come together and work for a world where there is no division of the races, and where people can move freely from place to place with no racial restrictions.

I was fascinated by him. He was so earnest. He spoke in a deep baritone voice, slowly as if each word is been weighed in his mind before it comes out of his mouth. He sounded so genuine and he spoke like no other white person I've heard before. It was an eye opener to me, learning and listening to two white people speaking about their world and their experiences of being white, privileged and educated. They said how sorry they were for all that white people are doing to Blacks, how angry it made them feel, and how fond they were of the Coloured and black people working in their kitchens and in their gardens. Both Sister Mary-Anthony and Mark said they got along well with the people from the townships, and Mark said they had only one maid who comes in to help his mother with the laundry once a week. I said we have no maids and my mother does her washing in two huge zinc tubs outside in the yard and my sisters and I muck in to help with the washing, but when I get my next pay cheque, I'm going to buy her a washing machine!

I don't remember much of the remainder of the evening, but I do remember rolling round in my bed later that night, not able to sleep: my mind was full to overflowing.

* * *

Over the next few weeks, I saw more and more of Mark and got to know him better as we worked side by side on different projects in the community. One day as we mixed cement and carried preformed blocks for a school building, I told him that it was a good thing that we hadn't met a year or two before, as I would almost certainly have greeted him by spitting in his face. He laughed and said that he wouldn't have blamed me! Nothing seemed to throw him.

I saw my family only once during those six weeks of intensive training. On our first 'free' weekend, I invited Mark home to meet my family. I shall never forget my Mum's reaction: "Jennifer, you can't be serious. How can you invite a white man to the house? You know it's house cleaning on a Saturday, and I want you to polish the front room floor, and there is the ironing to be done, and you must get your clothes ready for church tomorrow. What am I expected to give him to eat, you say he's a vegetarian? What is that?"

But it was my Dad who tore at my heart strings. He came in through the back door, wearing his white over coat, the uniform for drivers of Braam's Butchers & Meat Purveyors, carrying a box of cold meats that were past their 'sell-by dates'. I said: "Dada this is my friend Mark; he's having lunch with us today." My dear father put the box on the table when he saw Mark and wiped his hands on the front of his coat. "Pleased to meet you, master," he said when I introduced them. This was the subordinate manner in which those who are not white addressed white people, and I wanted to cry with embarrassment. I wanted the earth to open up and swallow me. But Mark opened his arms and hugged my Dad to him: "Pleased to meet you, Sir, I'm Mark. Can I call you Dada like Jenni does?"

That was the moment Mark revealed to me his soul: humble, kind, clear about who he is and what he's about, living out what he believes to be true and right. I loved him so much in that moment. How I loved the fearless, compassionate, humble, and beautiful human being who loved me with a deep love and with such shining pride all over his face when he looked at me.

Mum brought food to the table and even now – many years later – I cringe for our ignorance and for the harm we caused, unwittingly, to Mark that day! My poor Mum had no clue what vegetarian meant (later, she did say she knew he would not eat meat) so she fried onions with tomatoes and added eggs to it. Then she topped up the 'vegetarian dish' with a pinch of hot spices. Very politely Mark said thank you, and he started to eat. After a little while he began to turn a blue-ish colour and his face swelled up. He managed to stammer: "Doctor, get doctor." Mortified my parents and I realised that it had something to do with the food we gave him; something was very wrong. We phoned our local doctor who wasn't in surgery, but the receptionist told me that we must take Mark immediately to the nearest out-patients department at a hospital.

My dear Dad, still in his white coat, drove like a maniac to Constantia Berg hospital. He had the sense of mind to park near the entrance. I stayed in the car, as my Dad struggled with Mark dangling over him, disappeared through the entrance that said "Whites only". At the door, they let him in, thinking he was Mark's chauffeur! Poor Mark had an allergic reaction to the eggs. He was a pure vegan, but since he had just met my mother for the first time, and knew in his heart that her offering food was her way of welcoming him, he kept quiet and graciously accepted what she put before him. Since that incident I have learnt a lot about vegetarianism and vegans, and was myself attracted to a no meat diet.

My relationship with Mark continued to grow, but it was a relationship fraught with tension, hurt, social restriction, and political repercussions. Our relationship was also loving, exciting, fun and life-giving! We became savvy in our disguises and found creative ways to meet and 'date', but that had to be planned well in advance. We had to learn very quickly how to play the apartheid system at its own game. Most of our courtship happened in mass meetings or demonstrations in the streets – or in church!

* * *

Our first 'date' was attending a political rally in Mitchells Plain Civic Centre. A large crowd gathered from all walks of life and all colours of the rainbow. This happened three years before the launch of the United Democratic Front (UDF). The UDF was an organisation formed in 1983 comprised of civic bodies, community organisations, churches, mosques, businesses and individuals. It was a platform of the people for the people to speak out and act together against the illegal South African regime and their apartheid system. Like many other young people of my generation during the 1970s – 1980s, I got swept up in the new community politics and the revolutionary zeal that pervaded our meetings and social life. This was the time of heated discussions, political awakening for many Coloured youngsters.

Mark and I went to the Rally together, but he had to leave part way through, and promised that he would return before the rally ended to take me back home. After the Rally, I found him waiting for me in the car park. We decided to go for an ice cream before he dropped me off at home.

We walked down the Main Road in Kenilworth, each licking an ice cream cone. I was conscious of people staring at us with disapproval; I was aware that even those driving their cars were staring. Then we heard a sudden, almighty crash and the terrified screams of people around us. A little Morris mini with two elderly white ladies had crashed into a lamp post. It wasn't very serious, the car just gently ambled onto the pavement and collided with the lamppost. They were in complete shock! They had been staring at us, fascinated at what their eyes were seeing, and did not watch where they were going!

We created quite a stir with our brazen flaunting of the laws of the land. Such an unusual sight, unheard of and unseen at the time! A handsome young white man, holding hands with a short, Coloured girl, eating ice creams together – in public! No shame! No fear! In Kenilworth main road for all to see! This might be a common and normal scene anywhere else in the world, but not in apartheid South Africa. In the years that followed, wherever we went, we were the centre of stage whispers, fingers pointing and sometimes outright racism from members of the white community.

I remember one man walking up to Mark and telling him that he, Mark, was an embarrassment to the white community. How dare he flaunt his '*Hotnot meid*' for all the world to see? There are so many pretty blond white girls around. Can't he open his eyes? My Mark stood tall and stared the man in the face and said: "Excuse me, my lady and I are on our way to the beach, may we pass please?" And we swept past this racist bigot with his gaping mouth and the astonished onlookers as fast as we could. Sneers and embarrassed laughter followed us. I became used to the disapproving looks, surprised looks and fearful looks whenever we happen to be seen in public places.

* * *

And it was not just the Whites who did not approve of our relationship.

Mark didn't own a car when we first met, but he was allowed to borrow his Dad's blue Volkswagen, especially when we had to attend meetings further afield. At one time when his Dad needed the car, Mark came to fetch me at home and take me for a walk along the beach in Muizenberg. We left my home and boarded the train together. He had his arm around my shoulder. It was a crime for me to sit in a train carriage for 'Whites Only', so Mark stepped into the second class carriage with me. The train was full, but I managed to find a seat, hoping that Mark would remain standing near the exit doors. Instead, he followed me into the middle of the carriage and promptly knelt at my feet, facing me so that he could continue talking to me, looking up into my face, with his hands resting in my lap.

There was a lot of sniggering around; some of the Coloured girls in the carriage made loud remarks, "Who does she think she is? Look how black she is, she's not even pretty, *maar will ook wit piel hê* (but she also wants to taste a piece of white cock)!" It was vile, dreadful and very derogatory, and I felt myself burning with shame and feeling embarrassed about my looks, which had always been a problem for me. I didn't know where to look – while Mark seemed oblivious to the consternation we caused all around us. One of the men looked straight at me and said, "Oh girl, *jy gaan virrie gorilla* act" – "girl you are going to jail under the immorality act." The Immorality Act was one of the laws in South Africa which forbids any sexual intercourse between a white and a black/Coloured/Indian person.

We were entering Lakeside station when the ticket collector came along and demanded to see our tickets. He saw Mark still kneeling in front of me and told him to go and sit in 'his' carriage. Mark said 'Okay', but remained where he was. Another man said "*hey whitie, wat maak jy hier?* "Hey whitey, what are you doing here? Do you want a piece of brown meat – it's *lekka, nê!*" (brown meat is nice, hey?). Other passengers laughed outright, and made offensive remarks about white men and coloured women having nice caramel babies!

The ticket collector looked grave and pointed his finger at Mark and warned when he comes back and Mark is still in this carriage, he will slap a fine of R15 on him for travelling in the wrong carriage. When we got off at Muizenberg station, the train guard was standing on the platform, waiting for us. He kept the train waiting while he wrote out a fine and told Mark to go and pay in at the ticket office on the station, or risk going to jail for breaking the law. 'What law?' asked Mark, but the guard blew his whistle, jumped back into the train, and by this time every window and door had a body or a face peering from it. Some with curious expressions, mouths open, looking shocked; a few people were openly laughing, shouting obscenities with varying degrees of seriousness and support for us. Many others just stared at us – bewildered and bemused by what was happening in front of their eyes.

* * *

Angry Love

One evening Mark and I were on our way home from a 'Guerrilla Concert'. In those days we would act out real life scenarios (a domestic worker in the white madam's house, or a group of black miners coming home from work, or students in a class room, etc.) and draw out the social and political lessons. We performed outside supermarkets, or at the bus stops where there is always a queue of people. This kind of performances provoked heated remarks and on the spot dialogue between on lookers and 'actors'. They were performances that made people to look at themselves, how they behave, the way they live, but most of all it was a form of conscientization – using familiar every day scenes to raise awareness of how destructive the apartheid system truly is.

Anyway, one night, it was after eleven o'clock as Mark was driving the car through the quiet streets of the white suburb of Claremont, when we heard the police siren behind us, and a voice in Afrikaans, calling over the loud speaker, "Pull over; pull over, please." Mark pulled to the side of the road and this burly, red-faced policeman demanded in a loud voice, "*En waar gaan jy met die hotnot meid?*" (Where are you going with this Coloured servant?) Fortunately, I was still wearing the clothes I performed in, that of a domestic worker, blue overalls with a white apron and old takkies (sneakers). Mark turned down the car window and said in a clear strong voice, "I'm taking my la......" I jumped in and said in Afrikaans in a little girlie voice dripping with respect, "*Ag, my baas*, I work for his mother and she had a party, so young *baas* is just taking me home."

I knew from experience that if I appeared simple and submissive, that would be less likely to lead to a confrontation with anyone in a position of authority. So, I played the part, this sickening charade, to get us out of a situation that had the potential to turn nasty, with me possibly being taken to a prison cell for being with a white man alone in a car almost in the middle of the night. Mark would have had to pay a hefty fine, or worse, he could be charged under that monstrous "Immorality Act". The policeman peered into the car, saw me in my servant's uniform, and said, "Okay, move; drive on. We will follow you."

Mark looked at me, despair in his eyes, shrugged his shoulders and started the car. We drove in silence. Just before we got to my home, he said, "I was going to tell the bastard that you are my girlfriend. That I'm taking my lady home. I'm not ashamed of you, Jen." "I know, I know sweetheart, that's why I jumped in using the only language he will understand. We'll talk tomorrow. Thank you for bringing me home safely."

I so much wanted to lean over and kiss him, kiss away his unspoken apology, the guilt he felt for being white. I wanted to kiss away this humiliating experience, kiss away his pain – and mine. But the police man was again walking towards us. I opened the door and jumped out, ran to my front door before he could say a word to me.

My mother, who always sat and watched through the window for our safe return, immediately opened the door just as I was about to knock. I flew in, almost knocking her over. She saw the flickering blue light of the police van! "Jennifer, what happened? Why are the police outside? *Ai*, Jennifer, how many times must I tell you to leave these things. He's a white man; can't you see nothing can come from this nonsense?" "Mummy, stop; please stop now", I answered back almost in tears. "Nothing happened. The police just followed us all the way from Claremont, they just want to make sure we don't kiss, or something. They just want to show who's boss, that's all." My mother said, "You talk nonsense and you know that. 'They' rule our whole life; 'they' can put you in prison and what then, heh? What then? All your learning and education puff into thin air. What for? For a white man? *Moenie skande op ons bring nie* (Don't bring shame on us). Use your common sense, my girl! You want to tell me there's no-one else, no nice Coloured boys who can bring you home?" "Mummy, please, please don't go on; nothing happened. Mark only gave me a lift home after the concert! I'm going to bed. Night, night. Thanks for waiting up for me. "Lord help us," I heard my mother whisper.

* * *

Another time, Mark went to church with me. After church we walked to the bus stop to catch a bus to my home. There weren't many in the queue as it was a Sunday. Again, another police patrol van stopped right in front of us. "What are you doing here, young man?" the police man asked Mark. "I'm taking my lady home. We've just been to church" – and he showed his hymn book. The police man gave a snort and derisive laugh. "Your lady *nê*? This golliwog, your lady! Well, YOUR LADY can *innie fokking bus klim* and *jy kom met ons, meneertjie!*" He grabbed Mark by the arm. Mark's face was like granite. "Please let go of my arm," he said. "Mark, please, please just go. Just go with them. Don't worry about me. I'll be okay," I begged.

Others in the queue started sniggering. Someone said very loudly; *"Ja, julle Coloured meisies dink mos julle kak stink nie as julle 'n wit man het!"* (You coloured girls think your shit don't stink because you have a white man!). I didn't know where to look. So much vulgarity! I wanted to cry. The van drove off with Mark in the front seat, next to the white police driver. I kept my head down until the bus arrived.

* * *

Ours was not an easy courtship. There were few if any public places where we could socialise and be relaxed. We went to the cinema in a Coloured area once, but too many whispers and too many shocked stares meant that there was not a second visit. We never went for a meal in a restaurant nor went to clubs. Walking on the beach was a safe and enjoyable date. Most public places would not let us in. We tried, oh how we tried, several times we were shown the door by 'nice sympathetic' restaurant managers who told us they must adhere to management's segregated policies if they wanted to keep their jobs.

I remember the supportive and kind hearted friends who allowed us to use their homes to meet in. Just to be able to meet one another required detailed planning, a whole process and the enlisted help of more than one person. We tried not to walk together into the same house. We had to devise a way so that we do end up in the same place but not enter it together. Mutual friends would let him through the house to the backyard, and he would jump over two neighbours' fences to meet with me two doors away. The process would be reversed as we left. These 'cloak and dagger' meetings had more to do with Mark's situation than our inter-racial relationship. Because Mark refused to do military training, the army police was on the lookout for him; we weren't sure when or where they will suddenly make an appearance, therefore at times Mark had to wear disguises in various forms. But that is Mark's story to tell.

Over time, Mark endeared himself to my relatives and soon became like just one of the brothers in the house. My parents loved him and if they had reservations, it was not about our relationship with each other, but fear and concern about the political situation in which our love was growing. My siblings accepted him unconditionally. He teased and cajoled my younger sisters endlessly. And we spent many an evening sitting round the table in the kitchen helping the younger ones with their homework.

My meeting with Mark's parents was rather different. I visited Mark's parents' home twice during those early days, and I will never forget the first time I met his mother. She came through to the front door as Mark opened and called out, "We're here Mum!" She was wiping her hands on her apron and her eyes went round and her mouth opened into an *ohh* as she ushered us in without taking my outstretched hand.

During the meal she turned to me, put her hand over mine and apologised for not greeting me properly. She added that I'm welcome to visit anytime. I discovered that 'Mummy Sweet' (Mark's surname was Sweet) was soft spoken and warm in her acceptance of me. She was a gentle and kind mother who valued the happiness of her son above the racial laws of South Africa. She was a special kind of person and over the years I grew to love and respect her.

After the meal Mark moved to the kitchen to help his mother with the washing up, and from where I was sitting in the lounge, I could hear them chatting and laughing, and knew that Mark shared a special relationship with his mother. His Dad and I didn't have much to say to each other. Left alone, we both felt ill at ease and there was a long uncomfortable silence that he broke after about ten minutes and asked me about my family, where I worked, and how I knew Mark. The conversation didn't flow. It was stilted. So, I got up and walked about the room, stopping to admire some photographs of the family hanging on the wall. As I enquired about them, the old man pointed out his parents (Mark's paternal grandparents), his sister and Mark's elder brother. Dad Sweet was not inclined to make small talk and I sense he was struggling with my presence in his house, so I wandered outside into the garden. Luckily Mark soon appeared outside and suggested we leave and take a drive up to Chapman's Peak. I was happy to agree and felt a sense of relief when we were finally alone, in the car.

I went to Mark's family home one more time, and that was to say goodbye to Mark's mother, just before I left for England. I was glad Dad Sweet was not there because after that first meal with his family, Mark's Dad had taken him to task for breaking the law of the land. "*Soort soek soort* (like begat like)," he said. Look at the animals in the wild. They will all come to the same waterhole to drink, graze in the fields together, but at night the lion will go with the lion, and the monkeys with the monkeys. Why does he (Mark) want to mix things up and create confusion?" He said to Mark that I'm a likeable person and he's got nothing against Coloured people, but can Mark please think of the future and the awful repercussions if he continues with this 'silly' entanglement?

I suppose any white South African parent would react the way Mark's Dad did when a son brings a Coloured woman to lunch, and makes it quite clear that this is not just a frivolous fling, but an honest, loving relationship that is worth pursuing. Over the ensuing years during our marriage, Dad Sweet visited us twice in Notting Hill and we spent many pleasant times together. I grew to like him and I suppose he 'grew on me' – he introduced me to his acquaintances as 'my daughter-in-law' without any sign of prejudice or embarrassment. Here in England, we were just a normal family.

* * *

I pondered over our relationship a lot during those days, its uniqueness, and the danger attached to such a liaison. I was deeply in love with a man whom I admired and who added to my political and spiritual growth. But in apartheid South Africa our kind of relationship was labelled "Immoral and Illegal"; it was A CRIME, punishable with imprisonment or a hefty fine. Ours was not a 'normal courtship', because we lived in an abnormal society where *love had a colour*. In apartheid South Africa, you were allowed to fall in love only with a person who is the same colour as you are; but the heart does not know about that absurd law!

Angry Love

Chapter 3

Seeking Justice; getting glimpses of Grace

People often speak of conversion as a once-off experience, a Damascus Road experience like that of Saul, reported in the Book of the Acts of the Apostles. I have learned that conversion can also be a more gradual experience, less dramatic, but still life-changing; and I have learned that there can be several times of conversion throughout our lives. I think we are 'converted' every day when we are challenged to change our preconceptions of others, or when we are faced with buying clothes made on the exploitation of children in India. Working in the church and in the community in South Africa during the 1970s, I experienced several 'conversion experiences' – the most significant one was when I was picked up after one of my literacy sessions, and locked up in the local police station.

I was not conscious at that time of how my way of thinking was being changed, but looking back, I can see how, over a period of time, social justice became increasingly important to me, and the rules and practices and expectations of the Church, less so.

Seeing things differently

The Training Course I attended in Durban in 1976 marked an important stage in my growing consciousness of the damaging and all-pervading nature of Apartheid, and it made me become more active in the struggle to bring about transformation in my homeland. Holding together faith and politics became the framework of my life.

I have been asked many times how that was possible, and whether it was justifiable. I can only say that for me it was because of my following Jesus that I became so heavily involved in political action. The teaching of Jesus looks quite different when seen through the eyes of a woman of Colour, living under an illegal, oppressive regime. Growing up in a country governed by inhuman laws based on race, my faith propelled me into fighting for the right to be treated with dignity and to be treated as a human being. The United Nations described Apartheid as a crime against humanity; how could I *not* resist such criminal activity?

As a Community Development Worker, I saw how human lives were being eroded, and even destroyed by the institutional racism and racist economic policies inherent in the apartheid system. I was deeply concerned about the lack of education for our young people on the farms and subsequently discovered that there were many adults who was unable to write or read. My heart was grieved and I felt burdened with the conviction that I had to do something. But what, I did not know. So, I did what I was taught to do and what I believe is right to do: I prayed. I asked the Lord to show me what and how I could help 'the least of these' that he spoke about in Scripture.

Then one day it dawned on me: Teach them to read and write! I have never regretted responding to that inner voice, because I saw the benefit it brought to so many people over the years; and even though this activity was to lead later to my being imprisoned, I think that was a price worth paying.

Alongside my involvement in literacy, I developed a deeper awareness of the role of women, both in everyday life and in the struggle for justice. The person who helped me to see things in this new way was a young Jewish woman, Shelly Sachs, who was one of the contributors to our 'Alternative School'. She made me aware of the triple pressures we faced – as women; as workers (providing a readily available source of cheap labour); and as black people, who were regarded as not fully human. These insights helped to strengthen my commitment to working for justice and to shape my approach from then on.

For many people all around the world, Apartheid was perceived as a system that divided black from white, but Apartheid was more than that. Apartheid was a deliberate, legally enforced system of genocide. Every aspect of our lives was affected by this inhumane system: where we lived, where we went to school, the jobs we were allowed to apply for, even who you should marry! Women were involved in specific campaigns against racial and sexual discrimination. Indian, white and Coloured women took part in a march to Pretoria, protesting against the Pass Laws.

What I remember to this day is what Shelley told us in one of her sessions, about Dr Van Niekerk, an Afrikaner, who was a Member of Parliament in the 1960s. He sent out a questionnaire to all the advocates and legal professionals about the racial aspect of the death sentence. One advocate responded in Afrikaans: "I do not regard discrimination as unfair. Let us take the example of the rape of a woman. The Blacks are different from the Whites, that's how it is. For a white woman, rape, particularly by a black man, is a terrible experience. He must get the death sentence, I say. For the majority of black women rape by a white man is something which can be compensated for with a payment of cattle or a bag of mielies (maize)."

For me it was unimaginable that anyone could say anything so brutal and inhumane: I was shocked to the core as I listened to Shelly. But this is just one example of how black women were being perceived by racist white men, and also how non-white women had no legal platform to fight from. I became conscientized; I felt anger and determination simultaneously, and it became even more important to me that I should speak out and organise around the particular oppression of women.

I have seen old women, of no more use to the economy of South Africa, who are forced to live under inhuman conditions in the dry barren land of the Bantustans. Women of working age who live in those areas are treated as 'foreigners' and need permits to come and work in South Africa, where, as Black women, they are then subjected to the daily injustice of racist laws.

Building Community

While I will always remember the training course as the place where I first met Mark; it was very valuable in other ways too! It provided us with the basics of sociology, health care in the community, the demographics of Cape Town, and existing social networks around the Cape Peninsula. We studied and discussed concrete examples of how community development as a tool for change could enable and empower poor and dispossessed people, and how we as community developers could help build stronger, more cohesive communities.

One of the lecturers introduced us to the non-violent teachings of Ghandi and showed us how, if we chose to follow this method, we could achieve a better, more harmonious society in South Africa. He emphasised the need for us, as community developers, to listen with sensitivity to the people in the communities; to listen and hear what they say, and also what they do not say in words. He cautioned that we should always be aware that we are the ones coming from the outside into an established community, and, therefore, to have respect for those who have proven themselves to be the leaders among the people, and who have earned the respect of the community; they could become our allies and co-workers.

I kept this advice in mind when, during the last month of the training, we were thrown in at the deep end. Each of us was given R100 and then dropped off in one of the shanty towns dotted across the Cape Peninsula. Equipped with a backpack stuffed with our clothes, a note book, and toiletries, we were instructed to find a place where we could board and eat for a month! We also carried a letter bearing the stamp of the Churches Urban Planning Commission, our name and what we were about. It was a frightening experience to find myself in unfamiliar territory among a community of strangers – but that itself was an important part of the learning experience. The remit was very clear; we were to:
- Walk around and observe what was happening around us in the community;
- Actively participate by attending whatever civic meetings, political rallies, or church activities that were taking place;
- Go into as many homes as possible and talk to families about the things that mattered to them and how they manage to survive;
- Visit local schools and clinics.

We were expected to engage ourselves fully in the life of the community, and help them to help themselves in solving problems, becoming more self-sufficient and building stronger communities.

It was hard work and I learnt a lot about poverty, about single parenthood, about drink and drug related issues, and about myself. I discovered that every area of life is political – even buying a loaf of bread is political.

I did not have much self-esteem or confidence. But incredibly, my confidence grew. Day by day I walked on my own, talked to kids playing in the streets, walked with mothers to the shops, or on their way to the train station. Many a Monday morning I found myself sitting in the clinic with a woman who had been physically abused by her husband or boyfriend over the weekend.

One such woman was Mercia, who lived with an abuser for eight years. He would always swear undying love to her, and always promised that he would never beat her ever again. But I remember on two occasions holding her as she leaned against me with gashes on her arms and face, taking slow painful steps to the clinic. I asked her why she didn't call the police when her husband did these things to her? She said: "They will lock him up (when, or if, they do come); he will lose his job and who would then provide for her and her children, what will they eat, who will pay the rent? What she earns as a daily cleaner is just about enough for bus fares and bread to make school sandwiches for the children. Buying a loaf of bread is political.

Hers was a story typical of many households in that community. Manenberg was one of those gang controlled, poverty-stricken places with not much going for anybody; drug dealers ruled; there were no green parks, theatres or cinemas, or even a communal playground for the children. Most of the people lived below the bread line and for every second household of eight, there was only one wage earner.

* * *

In Manenberg, there also lived many decent people who had aspirations and tried to improve their lives. I found myself a place to sleep with a single mother and her three children. She asked me if I would mind sleeping with the children, as they lived in a two bedroomed council house. That was fine with me. I was no stranger to sharing a bedroom; I had shared one with my five sisters most of my life until then.

I spent a number of years working as Community Development Worker for the Churches Urban Planning Commission, which was based in Hanover Park, one of the poorest areas in the Western Cape. Even basic amenities did not exist, and families lived below the bread line, parents either working as domestic workers, factory workers, Council workers. During this time, we set up Cell Groups in Churches, formed 'Court' Committees (for blocks of flats) and organised community meetings, and ran a successful 'alternative school' twice a year.

The alternative school was initiated by Mark and two other workers, and young people from Hanover Park, Manenberg and Bonteheuwel were encouraged to attend. The sessions were held at a small Training Centre called Dora Falke, situated on a large piece of land between a road leading nowhere at the back, and in front of us the rolling beach of Muizenberg. This property belonged to the Methodist Church and was used for training purposes by different groups from all the denominations. There we discussed the Freedom Charter and what it would mean for South Africans to live out those ideals enshrined in the Charter. The names of some young people from the Bonteheuwel Youth Club who attended I recall vaguely as Ashley Kriel, Quentin Michaels and Ashley Forbes. Some became militant activists in the Liberation Movement and were at the forefront of the Street Committees that were formed in the early 1980s.

We were fortunate at the time, to have the input of Sociology students from University of Cape Town and teachers from the local schools who gave of their time voluntarily to teach us our own history of the indigenous Khoi San people. We learnt about the formation of the African National Congress (ANC) and leaflets about the South African Communist Party would also find their way into our notebooks. It was also on one of these Winter Schools that I learned about the Palestine Liberation Organisation (PLO) and the role of Yasser Arafat; I learned also about Sinn Fein, and heard the name Che Guevara for the first time.

New insights and knowledge found their way into my hungry mind and the more informed I became, the more outspoken I became against the apartheid system.

Conscientization

One of my particular passions was using literacy in the way that Paolo Friere pioneered its use, as a tool for conscientization and, eventually, liberation. This technique is contextual and is designed to create critical consciousness in the minds of recipients. In this method of teaching, we used 'codes', a collage or a drawing of an everyday scene that would be familiar to the group. It might be, for example, a picture of a group of women bent over their machines in a clothing factory.

The teacher asks an easy opening question: What are they doing? Answer: they are sewing dresses. For whom? For customers to come and buy in the big shops. Question: What is the price of one dress in the shop? Answer: R300. Question: How many dresses does one machinist make in one day? Answer: about 24. Question: So, if one woman makes 24 dresses at R300 each, how much money is that? Answer: [a lot!]. Question: Who gets this money? Answer: The white bosses! Question: how much does the worker get paid, what would be your wages? Answer: R550 per week. So, what is happening here? "You, the workers, must work, day in day out, for this pittance. You are in cramped conditions, and restricted to not more than 7 mins in the toilet; your wages are so little, and the bosses take the bulk of this money created by your labour." We found that workers learned much more quickly, when the words they were taught to read and to write related to their real-life situations!

The small groups of adults I taught became critically conscious in such a life-affirming and liberating way. From some of the more outspoken women I heard of the gradual emergence of grassroots resistance movements that started to shoot up in small pockets across the Western Cape. I was able, as a Community Development Worker, to travel around and taught farm workers, domestic workers and factory workers to read and write, always starting with their real-life situations. It was a moving experience to see how people start to believe in themselves once they can read. They begin to believe that they can make a difference in their lives, that even 'insignificant' people like them, can be part of bringing about change.

I saw it in the way women in one factory started walking taller and began to speak more confidently to their Line Manager. Observing this powerful change in ordinary people, was exhilarating for me. I remember how one of the older men cried when at sixty years of age, he wrote his name for the first time. But teaching literacy, especially in this way, was seen as "subversive education" by the apartheid regime, and it was for that I was later put into prison.

But before then, it was a heady time, a time of deep emotions and new learning, a time in which I grew politically and spiritually. A time in which I became part of a wider family and my birth family saw less and less of me.

* * *

I met women who belonged to the Federation of SA Women (FEDSAW), an organisation that linked women's issues firmly with the struggle against apartheid laws. Their refrain which became mine too, was: "We are women; we are workers; we stand together." It was from them that I learnt about the huge march to Pretoria in 1955, where the women handed in petitions against the pass laws. All through their lives these women had experienced and witnessed the effect of pass laws on their men: the night raids, being stopped in the street at random by police vans, and the ongoing persecutions.

I also assisted another women's organisation, the Black Sash, by doing a survey about women in the resettlement areas, particular in the Cape. I discovered that when first relocated, a family would be supplied with a 9x9m zinc structure, oven hot in summer, and ice box cold in winter. This needed to be insulated, floored and extended. Communal toilets were erected a distance away. I remember helping to carry water from a communal tap – everything had to be carried: water in containers, wood from the surrounding areas, household supplies, including paraffin for the primus stove, from the shop 6km away.

It was a hard life, exacerbated by the absence of the fathers and the grown-up sons in the household. These women never lost their faith or the hope "that tomorrow, next year, when my child is grown up, life will be better." They inspired me and they taught me that Jesus is to be found and loved in and among women who have no home to call their own, women who, after a storm, or after the bulldozers come and destroy their little shacks, are forced to painstakingly begin to build their homes of tin, hessian, wood, newspaper and zinc. These women taught me lessons I shall never forget.

What really matters

One of the most endearing memories I carry with me was of the day when I walked into an area called Cross Roads; the bulldozers, accompanied by the police, had just left the area that morning. In the afternoon, as I was preparing to leave the area, I was stopped by a little girl. "Auntie Jenni, come; my Mama call you to my party! It's my birthday. Today I am six years old." I followed her to a small rickety shack, blowing perilously in the wind. Inside this one roomed shack, stood 3 other women around a small round table on which was laid a white table cloth. In the middle was placed an enamel plate filled with *vetkoek* (a round dumpling filled with jam).

The mother of this little girl worked as a domestic worker in Sea Point, and her employer had given her a tin of red fruit jam. She used this and some flour given to her by a neighbour, to fry these delicious sweet cakes in honour of her daughter's sixth birthday! I felt so humble. I was so deeply stirred as well as immensely proud at that moment to be part of this small gathering of brave, and beautiful women who can still find joy and laughter in such dire and poverty-stricken surroundings. Since then, I have attended many children's parties: parties with a jungle theme, parties with a frozen theme, parties where girls and boys come dressed up as kings and queens, or as their favourite TV character... but *that* party on that day in Cross Roads, was the real thing – a true celebration of life; even though *that* life was lived in unacceptable conditions in a wood and tin shack on a windswept no-man's land.

* * *

In 1977, I went to serve as a Community Development Worker attached to the Methodist Children's Home in Vryburg, a small village near Potchefstroom in the Northern Cape. One day I was asked by one of the women who attended my literacy classes to accompany her to the cemetery. She explained that this day would have been the thirtieth birthday of her daughter, who had died some ten years earlier. I stood with her beside the grave, which had a slate tombstone, on which was written, "Mother and Child lie buried here."

With tears in her eyes, this grandmother told me the story: Her daughter, at the age of 19, was working as a maid in one of the big hotels in Cape Town. There she met a young white man, and they fell in love with each other. Because the apartheid laws of the land prohibited black and white from getting married legally, they decided to live together in secret as husband and wife. During the day she pretended to be his domestic worker by wearing a maid's uniform that indicated her status as a domestic worker, so that she could accompany him to the supermarkets. One day he met with a tragic accident and was killed on his motor bike.

When Maria, the daughter, discovered that she was pregnant, she came back to live with her parents in Vryburg. When the child was born, it was very light skinned and had light eyes, but with African hair. Since this was a predominantly white Afrikaner community, people became antagonistic towards the mother and child whenever they walked in the local town; they started pelting them with stones and made life very difficult for Maria and her mixed-race daughter. Time passed; life became increasingly difficult and more and more things happened that isolated this family from the rest of the community. Eventually, one night, someone came and threw petrol around the zinc hut in which they lived, lit a match and the little shack and everyone inside fast asleep burned to death – mercifully, the grandmother was not in the hut at the time.

It is a tragic story, but sadly, not so strange in South Africa, where tales of racism, hatred, bigotry, inhumanity and intolerance are told repeatedly. It is a tragic story, about what human beings can do to each other when they are indoctrinated with evil. This grandmother, one of my star pupils, started the first multi-racial crèche in Vryburg. In my time there, she welcomed little black babies and little white toddlers because she said she does not want the same thing to happen to other children growing up in the same village ever again. I still hear her words to me, reverberating over the decades since this happened: "Our children must grow up, knowing and believing that we are all equal before God, and that they all have the same worth as a human being."

The Way of the Cross?

Deep in my heart I believed that Apartheid was wrong, and hearing stories like Maria's convinced me that the apartheid system treated black people as not-human, not having human feelings and emotions. A slow anger began to manifest itself in my chest, and it was not long before that slow anger grew into a full fierce blaze – and in my blazing anger I swore at God.

It was that day when I was sitting on a bus which had come to a halt because of a protest march by students from the local schools. I saw a boy, about eight years old, running down a dusty road with an empty paraffin bottle in his hand; I imagined that his mother had sent him to the corner shop to buy some paraffin for their primus stove.

The South African police and riot squad were out in full force, as happened increasingly when there were student protests, and as usual, they started to fire indiscriminately into the crowd (birdshot, they said afterwards); they spurted tear gas all over the protesters and by-standers, and used their dogs to harass and intimidate them. From my vantage point on the bus, I saw people running helter-skelter in all directions: into shops and driveways; some climbing up the trees that lined the road.

A cloudy mist was hanging over everything, and then I saw the little boy running towards the bus, his eyes wide open and panic written all over his face. It was a hot sunny day and he was clad in only in his shorts. Neither I, nor any of the other passengers on the bus realised that he had been shot – until I saw his stomach slowly open up like a zip being pulled by an unseen hand. I saw blood coming first from a tiny hole, and then the blood seems to spurt out like little fountains right down his tummy. The little one stood still, mouth gaping, eyes wide and round filled with terror. He swerved aside, stumbled away from the bus and plunged further along the dusty road.

We watched in horror and saw him lift his head once; saw his mouth moving, but could not hear any sound because of all the noise and confusion both outside and inside the bus. By now we were all shouting and myself and two other women jumped out and ran to towards the little boy. Outside near the body, we were stopped by a policeman holding out his gun towards us: "No, no", he said, "You cannot touch that child. Is he yours?" "No," we answered. "Then move away, go away. We will deal with this terrorist! LEAVE!"

I stared at this man. His eyes hard and full of hate. I looked down at the little boy with an empty paraffin bottle beside him. A terrorist? What I saw was a little child in pain, in agony, possibly dying; his leg twitched in the sand and I heard a sound like a wounded animal escaping from his lips. Now the blood was gushing out of his mouth in tiny bubbles. Dear God, oh my God help us I cried inside. "Maai." He cried like a cat. He was crying for his mother; he needed his mother. And then, there was silence. Just a second of silence in that maelstrom of noise and babble.

It was then I swore at God. I lifted my face to the sky and from my guts I swore at God. I uttered expletives that I wasn't aware that I knew. I swore at this white policeman in his blue uniform, his menacing gun pointing at me. I swore at the blue sky, at the sun shining down on us. "God, what is happening? Why, God? Why?"

This is but one of many experiences that convinced me there just is no other way to be a Christian in South Africa than to participate in the struggle against the inhuman, evil system of Apartheid. Where in the world will a little child be shot at when all he did was to run an errand for his Mum, going to the shop to buy paraffin so that they can light their primus to cook their food. Where in the world will an eight-year-old be called a terrorist? Does this little one even know what a terrorist is? Can he spell the word terrorist?

* * *

Suffering and struggle had become the norm for the majority. As black people in South Africa we were born into struggle and had to continue to struggle until Apartheid was overthrown. I could see no other option. Jesus said, "Greater love has no-one than this, that she gives her life for others." Jesus gave his life hanging on a cross; and the belief grew within me that there was no need to be afraid of the cross.

Later, I spoke to my friends in the church, and they said

we must pray and then things will change for the better. We did. But very little changed. To me it seemed things got worse when many of my activist friends were not able to live in their family homes for fear of visits from the security police. It was not long before I found myself in the same boat and I, too, left my mother's house. The main reason we lived away from home was to protect our families from being implicated in our political activities.

When a close family member was shot by the police during a demonstration and later died in hospital, I felt terrible because I was the one who had encouraged, even begged, him to take part in the demonstration. Alongside the guilt I felt for his untimely death, there was also a greater resolve to make a difference. That resolve took me into a world of pseudonyms and clandestine meetings, of codes and camouflage techniques – and learning to make Molotov Cocktails!

I became a member of the Black People's Convention (where I befriended Harold Dixon and Steve Carolus, whose sister, Cheryl, was the South African Ambassador in Britain in the 1990's) and we worked together with the Young Catholic Workers' Movement who produced inspiring written materials that we distributed in the clothing factories and motor industry around the country. These two organisations, with the support of South African Students Organisation (SASSO) and members of the Domestic Workers Union, organised a nationwide red meat boycott. This was in response to the high price of meat that the poor could not afford. Six of us went into a supermarket – I can't remember where now, or who was with me at the time – but I do remember filling up my trolley with red meat from the freezer, and the shelves. I then join the queue for the cashier to ring up my prepacked red meat bundles; the assistant packed them neatly into the Pick n Pay carrier bags and the cashier asked for my money. I did what the other five at different tills did – I refused to pay. I said I have no money, just like hundreds of people outside have no money to pay such high price for red meat. And before she could say anything further, I bolted out of the shop and ran for my life!

In Salt River, we printed a community newspaper called Grassroots. As a supplement we did an educational magazine for children called Molosongololo to create awareness among the very young. We distributed this on the Cape Flats, in Mitchells Plain and among high school pupils. In all those community resistance activities, I was never at the forefront. I was just another face in the crowd, but I felt part of the vibe, in solidarity with those who protest and with those who suffer

It was a fearful time, a time when anger spilt onto the streets; it was a time of boldness and solidarity, and it was also a time when spontaneous creativity burst forth from the most unlikely sources. It was a time when I felt most useful and humbly believed that my small contribution was of significance. And I remembered the words of Jesus: "Whoever wants to be my disciple, must take up the cross and follow me." I believe those words of our Lord Jesus inspired me and gave me courage.

In the factories dotted around the Western Cape, women worked as unskilled labourers, low paid and penalised if time is lost for illness or family emergencies. Pregnancy means the loss of your job, and for some women, it meant being packed off to a Bantustan. So when, during one of my literacy classes, the group of women factory workers who came to my sessions, told me that money is being deducted from their meagre wages if they stay in the toilet longer than seven minutes, we together worked on a plan of action. Early one winter morning, around seven o'clock, a group of women, dressed in their dark blue overalls and white *doeks* (head-scarves) marched silently down the road to the factory gates. The plan was that no-one is to enter the gates until one of the Management came out to receive the petition which we had drawn up:

- for better and safer working conditions;
- an appropriate length of time allowed in the toilet;
- these demands to be implemented at the beginning of next month;
- management must agree to these requests by signing it in front of all of us.

As we drew near to the gates which were still closed, we were surrounded, out of the blue by armed police. As one, the women knelt down in the road and started to pray loudly in the different languages – Afrikaans, English, Xhosa, Setswana and Zulu. I looked on in amazement, this was not in our plans and we hadn't even discussed an ambush like this! Can you imagine the scene! It was surreal! The white *doeks* women on their knees wailing and beseeching God to intervene, their faces lifted to the sky, arms outstretched up high; the big burly white police men standing with their guns in mid-air, baffled. The sun just beginning to filter through the trees, dappling the faces of some of them, making the women look like they have some kind of sheen on their skin. The factory siren started going off – howling through the cries of the women! It was so surreal.

* * *

I felt that God was there.

* * *

It took another four months before the bosses and management signed an agreement that stipulated a wage increase and no time restrictions on going to the loo. We were elated and felt some satisfaction, but I knew more needed to be done to bring about real justice. We were not just fighting for legal rights, but for a more humane life.

All over the country women, black, Coloured and Indian women were organising boycotts, took part in demonstrations, prayed in the churches, in mosques, in their homes. Women, not only black women, from all walks of life played a vital part in dismantling Apartheid. We worked together round the values enshrined in the Freedom Charter that "this land belongs to all who live and work in it; no government can claim authority unless it is based on the will of the people. We have been robbed of our birth right to land, liberty and peace by a government founded on injustice and inequality."

I lived in the belief that they can take away our lives, but they will never take away our humanity. This deep ingrained sense of humaneness was displayed when a well-known woman, Dr Mamphela Ramphele, set up a clinic and literacy projects in the Northern Transvaal. She was under banning order because of her association with Steve Biko, the Black Consciousness Leader who died in prison. In spite of being a banned person, she gave her skill and her energy so that 'others may live'.

I know many more who 'gave of themselves', among them I remember in particular, Godfrey, a white soldier who later became a conscientious objector, and helped Mark when he needed to get out of South Africa. Godfrey told me he was serving in the SADF when one particular day their commander told them to get ready and braced themselves to face the "swart gevaar" (the black danger). They were driven into a township where there was a public demonstration in progress. Along the way some of the soldiers were thirsty and stopped at the local café to buy cold drinks. Godfrey jumped down with his gun in its holster, and bent down to speak to a boy who was about fifteen years old. As he was talking to this young man, the commanding officer shouted at him to jump back onto the hippo (army truck).

Godfrey told me that as he jumped back onto the army vehicle, this nasty man pulled out his gun and shot the boy in the feet. He then calmly drove off and left the young man lying injured in the street! After this incident, Godfrey found the courage to do what he never thought possible: he left the army, said goodbye to his family and friends and escaped to Britain. Here he joined other white men in an organisation named COSWAR. They too, played a vital role in nurturing young white men who wanted to 'fight' for a world where there is no place for racism, no Apartheid and no killing of defenceless children.

* * *

The killing of school children in Soweto in 1976 made world headlines. The picture of Hector Petersen's dead body being carried in the arms of his friends, running away from the police with shock and anguish on their faces, went round the world. But that was just one picture in a long history of the suffering and brutality that black children had experienced – and continued to experience in the following years. It seems almost unbelievable that while the world saw all this, there are white South Africans who claimed to me in 1999, that they were not aware of any of these things at the time, and heard about them only much later! I think that many white South Africans really lived in another world!

The bravery of the youngsters in SOWETO spread across the country inspired more young people, and caused an outpouring of militancy and courage and activism all over Cape Town, Stellenbosch, Cradock and other areas in the Western Cape. The young people came out in force across the country, and the authorities responded with force: I lost count of how many funerals I attended at the time.

* * *

However, there was some solace to be found, I think, in the huge outcry from the church and ministers of religion who did not hesitate to voice their anger against the draconian apartheid laws, and in solidarity with their respective communities joined the many marches, and spoke at public meetings and in their sermons. Some prominent figures in the Church, Synagogue and Mosques made petitions to the government based on their faith beliefs; letters signed by these brave clergy found their way to government offices and some even had meetings with government officials.

Ordinary people started writing poetry and new songs were born – giving expression to the daily grind of exploitation and repression that was the hallmark of South African society.

Songs of lament and freedom filled the air and people were singing like never before in the street, in the church, in the train, singing their hearts out. Many were crying as they sang mournful, heart-breaking melodies. Whenever activists met, we always began with a chant of defiance or a hymn, with all of us singing from deep within our souls. It was not unusual for us to begin our meetings with tear-stained faces.

These were fearful times for those who believed that Apartheid is a crime against humanity. Many activists died or disappeared mysteriously, as the regime became desperate and started implementing one law after the other in an effort to frighten people and to deter the rising militancy and determination of ordinary people. Public meetings were banned. Many of our phones were bugged, and plain clothes police and informers would attend house gatherings openly. Even a normal birthday party did not escape the police presence! Every meeting was a potential danger sign to the regime and many more draconian laws were introduced.

One of those laws was the restriction on numbers attending a funeral service, because the regime discovered that the comrades were using funerals as a platform for consciousness raising and recruiting for the (ANC) underground movement. Emotions were running high and there was tangible tension in the air. The only place where we could still gather without hindrance was on a Sunday morning in church.

However, because police informers were everywhere, even in church, we had to devise ways of communicating that would be understood by only the people who needed information. So, for instance, when bus fares were increased suddenly to a level that people could not afford, it was decided that there should be a rolling boycott of buses and the way in which the targeted route was made known was by the number of the hymn that was announced by the minister at a particular point in the worship service.

In our weekly prayer meetings, we prayed loudly for families whose children were in prison for political activities, mentioning their names, but not surnames; informers came even to the prayer meetings – though not necessarily to pray. What I remember most from these gatherings were the poignant prayers and vulnerability that shone through when ordinary people called upon God, and had such innocent assurance that God was indeed listening to their lament.

One such prayer that have always stayed in my mind, and still brings a smile to my lips and tears to my eyes, was said by the father of a young boy who was in prison, and went something like this: "God in high heaven, look down upon this earth you have made and you will see all the terrible people. Some of them are just out to give you high blood pressure. Especially that man FW de Klerk. He is supposed to be our leader, ahhmm, I mean the white people's leader, but we also got him in the bargain. You know that man, but maybe when you made him, your thoughts were far away which made you not to pay much attention to what you were doing. But the Bible say you can change anybody if you want to; so, change him please. Speak to his brains and help him to see that we are of the same colour blood. Help Mister de Klerk to see how we suffer when he sits at the table with good food and we have nothing except bread and *pap* (cornmeal porridge). Maybe you don't know that he's a *blerrie* racist man who kill brown and black children. Let him die a gruesome death, Lord. Help us to force the politicians to make new laws of justice. Give us strength in our legs to walk to that prison tomorrow as we demand that this stupid government will release our children. For your sake, Amen." Those were times of utter vulnerability and almost comic honesty!

* * *

Holding together faith and political activism proved challenging sometimes. It was during 1978, soon after I completed my Local Preacher's Certificate, that I was approached by two young comrades carrying a tightly sealed brown box. They asked me if I could find a safe place to hide this box. "It is in the interest of the struggle", they said, and added earnestly that I must see it as part of my contribution to our freedom.

They explained: "We cannot hide it in our shacks in the Township, the police are everywhere. They just come bursting in through the doors and search every inch of our homes whenever they want to. You are a Christian, going to church and you are a Coloured woman who lives in a nice area. Please hide it somewhere until we ask you for it."

What could I do? Wasn't this an opportunity to show that I was fully committed to the struggle and that I wanted to follow the commission of Jesus to "free the oppressed, to give shelter to the homeless, to be a neighbour to those who cross my path"? I took the box, and went and hid it under the floorboards, right beneath the pulpit in the church!

Many years passed, and many things happened before I saw that box again, and when I did, I had to face again the challenge of holding together truth and justice, faith and political activism;

of being, in the words of Jesus, "as cunning as a snake, and yet as harmless as a dove". But that is an account for another time.

Imprisoned

In 1977 I was detained with several other activists around the country. The policeman who picked us up, wrote in his little book, "for promoting subversive education". I was never formally charged, or brought to trial in a court; I was just left in a cell for seven days. In that time, I went through my most profound experience of conversion. It was my first darkest hour ... and I was very afraid.

The whole ordeal of being locked up in a cell was like a horrible nightmare. I was separated from the other activists (of course they wouldn't keep us all together, we might start plotting together, and find a way to blow up the police station!) The first night was by far the worst, I was on my own, and I was afraid, really afraid, of what might happen to me: I'd heard from other comrades about being tortured and being stripped naked and forced to stand throughout the night under a bright light. I spent most of the first night crying.

I was afraid to sleep and I was afraid to stay awake, never knowing what is going to happen next. I was given a thin grey blanket to cover myself, no pillow; a tin bucket to wee in was standing in the corner. The cell smelled of damp and sweat and urine, and there were cockroaches everywhere; a bright light hung from the ceiling. I remember loud voices speaking in Afrikaans and bells ringing at odd times. This was a part of my life that I have tried to block out of my memory, and I actually do not remember much, but hazy flashbacks haunted me for many years and many a night I would wake up screaming.

The next few days were a bit of a blur. Breakfast each morning was half-cooked pap with an enamel mug of weak, cold, black tea. I do not remember much about what I was thinking at the time, or what I did, except I do remember every day counting the ants walking backwards and forwards on the cement floor, and that I repeated the Psalms every day. (Oh, how thankful I was for the days when my mother had forced me to read and memorise the Psalms – the words of lament, of praise, of frustration and anger all came back to me and I said them with new meaning.)

After being on my own for five days, I was joined in my cell by three other women; they were sex workers who had been arrested in a night club. I was still feeling very vulnerable and initially I was very wary of these women. They noticed how afraid and insecure I was – they could hardly help noticing as I cowered and snivelled in my corner of the cell! One of them took it on herself to try and strengthen me, encouraging me not to let the situation get me down. Gradually, we shared our stories. I learned sacred lessons from these women; sisterhood took on new and deeper meaning for me, and they changed me at a profound level. Another conversion, one of many!

Throughout my life I have found it almost impossible to settle down for the night without first saying my prayers; it is something that's deeply ingrained. So, each night in that crowded cell, I would try to find a way of saying a Psalm and praying, without making what I was doing too obvious. But of course, my cell mates saw what was happening and accepted it as part of who I was. Then they began asking me to pray for them and for the people who meant most to them; it was becoming a true 'Cell Group' with a difference, for I daresay not many religious cell groups would speak about a holy God and a male penis in the same breath! We laughed a lot as they recount their funny, ladies of the night's experiences and they made me into a more understanding and tolerant of their situation.

On the seventh day of my imprisonment, a policeman came to the cell and told me that I was to be released the next day. No explanation was given, and I hardly dared to believe what I had heard. That evening, as I prepared for my final night with my new community, one of them asked if I would do with them 'that thing that you Christians do.' I didn't have a clue what she was talking about. Then one of the other women explained that they would like me to share Communion with them. Now in church there are strict rules about who can and who cannot serve Communion, and in some churches, even rules about who can and who can't receive it. According to those rules there was no way that we could have Communion that night. But we did. And, looking back, I'm so glad we did.

It is a holy moment to sit in a prison cell with three people you have known for such a short time and in such painful circumstances; to sit with them, sharing a crust of old dry bread and an enamel mug with water that looked like it came from the toilet. Cockroaches were crawling around my legs and mice scurrying along the floor, but it was a holy moment as I whispered "This is my body; this is my blood." It was a moment too deep for words. Oh, how I wept! I still do, when I recall what has been for me the most powerful experience I have ever had of remembering Christ's death and the meaning of his love and resurrection.

Moving On

My Mum and Dad came to fetch me from the police station the morning I was released. I remember how they stood at first, just staring at me. Then my Mother cried out and ran and held me – and told me that I stank. My Dad just looked at me with tears in his eyes. All he said was, *"Ai Here tog!"* (Oh dear Lord). My parents told me never to speak about this incident in the house in front of my siblings, or to anyone else in the family, or with friends. They were ashamed that I had been put in prison. For my parents and people of their generation, if the police lock you up then you have done something wrong, not the police! So, I kept quiet, and never spoke to any in my community about my awful experience. Years later, my sister told me that I could've been released days earlier, but my parents didn't have the money to bail me out. During the time I was locked up, my parents was put in the humiliating position of having to go round to family members to borrow the bail money for my release, up to this day I don't know who the family members are who helped, and if they're still alive.

* * *

That year 1977, was a strange year for me when I lost much of what was a familiar pattern before I was locked up. I was not allowed back to teach in the Sunday School (I was told by our minister that parents were afraid that I would teach politics rather than the Bible to their children); I didn't want to see many of my friends and I hardly left the house, except for my work in the community.

In early 1979, Mark was able to move into a house in Woodstock and I went to live with him there. It was relatively safe for a mixed couple to live in that area, because Woodstock was one of those 'grey' suburbs where all colours of the rainbow rubbed shoulders on a daily basis. Our house was the place where students, and other activists would gather to discuss and debate way into the night. We held many '*goembas*' – a meeting with political aims under the guise of a social gathering – in Shannon Street, Woodstock.

I did not attend all the political meetings held in the house; I had a job that demanded an early start, but would always see that there was something to eat for those who travelled from as far afield as Stellenbosch and the Northern suburbs. It was during those late nights that a new militant group (however small in number), of young people was born – it was a time to dream of equality, freedom and losing the shackles of apartheid. All the young people who met in our home were involved with resistance activities in their local communities. Many of them had the added responsibility of earning money to support a family where either mother or father was in prison for their own political activities.

Apart from his role as tutor, Mark was also the driver and much of our pooled cash resources went in buying petrol to get people to their homes, or as happened on several occasions when discussions ran through the night, straight to their places of work. Mark was not afraid to drive by himself into the townships, and into areas that was seen to be 'unsafe' for a white person to be. He proved himself in all aspects to be a person that can be trusted, a brother to confide in, a friend who will cover your back, in short, a comrade who was loved and respected by his peers.

It was not unusual for Mark to be driving to Stellenbosch or Malmesbury at four o'clock in the morning, dropping off students at their respective homes, and then return to Cape Town with a car load of domestic workers. Each one would be driven right up to their employer's homes either in Sea Point or Bishops Court. For Mark this was all part of 'the struggle' – nothing was too menial or too small a task to do. I admired him all the more for his humility and sincerity. Our relationship grew more intimate and was strengthened by our commitment to free our people from the shackles of apartheid. I was so proud of him and my happiness to be known as 'his lady' knew no bounds.

In March 1979 we became engaged in a small hall in Square Hill, Retreat. Surrounded by a gathering of trusted friends, family and work colleagues, Mark asked me to marry him! Among our guests was the daughter of Nelson Mandela, Zindzi Mandela, who was brought along by comrade Ann Tomlinson. Zindzi did not stay for the party, she was enroute to another meeting. But for all that very brief encounter, it was a highlight for me to meet the young woman whose father was languishing on Robben Island and whose name was always mentioned with such respect by everyone.

But, as with so much that happened in South Africa at that time, that moment of our greatest happiness and hope was to be followed by agony not long afterwards.

Angry Love

Chapter 4
Leaving Home

My growing political consciousness and my 'forbidden love' relationship turned me into a restless, angry young woman, who became rather outspoken in the meetings of our Church Council, which were very usually conventional events. After one such meeting where I had again given vent to my feelings, the Minister came to me and said that he could see I needed to find some way to continue exploring my growing social awareness and that he had found a way to help me.

The South Africa Council of Churches Youth Desk and their Justice and Peace Desk were jointly organising a conference in which political and religious debate would come together, and they were inviting Churches to nominate youth leaders with a social conscience to take part in this open forum. At the next Church Council, the Minister put my name forward, and I was elected unanimously to represent our District at this 'one of its kind' week-long conference, to be held in Lesotho. Young people from all the different Provinces in Southern Africa attended, as well as members of SWAPO, the liberation movement of Namibia.

Upon my arrival I was given the programme for the week and was surprised to see my name down as a Chairperson for a day. Selected participants were chosen to chair the Programme each day. One of my duties was to introduce the Speaker for that particular day, who was none other than Archbishop Desmond Tutu. Before we started the proceedings, I had to approach him to find out about his life and interests so that I could present him to the Conference. This was one of those opportunities of a life time and I felt completely unprepared!

The Archbishop was welcoming and friendly; and he must have noticed my nervousness because he quickly put me at ease by telling me I would be his friend for life if I did not preface his name with 'Old Man'. I laughed, and emphatically declared that I would never dream of referring to him in such a way. So, there I sat next to this great man of God, duly performing my duties as the Chair, making notes, monitoring the questions (which he answered) and then, just as I was about to thank him on behalf of the whole Conference, he put up his hand as if to detain me.

He stood up next to me and courteously asked me, as Chair, for permission to speak! At my nod, he explained that among us there were also international visitors, and that in particular he would like to introduce the Rev Dr John Vincent from the Urban Theology Unit in Sheffield, England, who would like to address this Conference before I brought the day's proceedings to a close. Doctor Vincent was elegantly dressed, and he spoke eloquently about his venture that promoted "doing theology from the bottom up". He said that he was there in South Africa to extend an invitation to two young people to come to England and to study theology there for twelve months. He said, further, that he would only accept applications from young people who had the backing of their church, and a character reference from their minister, supporting their application.

John Vincent explained that the funding for the studies would come from the Overseas Division of the Methodist Church in Britain and would be available to the successful applicants once they had arrived in England, but that the students would have to be responsible for their own air fares to England, as this is not included in the grant from MCOD. He then turned to the Archbishop Tutu, handed over three large brown manila envelopes, and asked the Archbishop if he would kindly take this matter in hand to find the appropriate candidates among the Conference delegates.

During the evening meal I found myself again sitting next to Archbishop Tutu, and he encouraged me to take up John Vincent's invitation. When I subsequently confided that I did not have the means to buy a flight ticket to England, he made an astonishing offer, that the SACC would provide the money for my airfare, on condition that, on my return, I would give something back, in particular to the work of the SACC. I was humbled that someone in Desmond Tutu's position had seen me as a person worthy to be given such an opportunity.

I returned to Cape Town, hardly daring to believe that all this had happened and that, perhaps, I could be leaving my homeland in a little while. It all began to seem more real when a few months after the Conference the Treasurer of my home church reported that a sum had been deposited into the church account, sufficient to cover all my travel expenses. The news was received by my family with joy and excitement, and the church community was overjoyed when the news spread, like wildfire, and they heard that I had been accepted by a College in England and that I would be going there to study Theology.

* * *

Now, there is one thing that you must know about South Africans, before I go any further: greetings and partings are matters requiring great care. A quick 'Hi' on entering a home, even the home of a family member, or a speedy 'Bye' when leaving, is never acceptable; each person present must be given proper attention and a suitable greeting. Imagine, then, what it was like to say farewell to someone who was going, not just round the corner to their own home, but far away for at least a year! My farewells were spread over several events and several weeks.

The first farewell was arranged by the church choir. About 60 people turned up with gifts, cakes and there was much laughter. The choir sang my favourite hymn, "God will take care of you", and we cried, and hugged one another with deep affection. Everyone promised to pray for me. And I promised to write to each one. I wrote one letter once.

Then there was the Sunday School Staff and a few of the children. They organised a curry evening and all who came brought a dish of curry to the Church Hall. We formed a circle holding hands and prayed. We sang again "God will take care of you", the hymn that accompanied me right through my spiritual journey. This is the hymn that gives me assurance and I draw deep strength from it. The third farewell party was when the Ladies Fellowship organised a "High Tea", South African style, with yellow rice and bobotie looking colourful among the butterfly cakes and scones. Up to this day I have in my possession crocheted gloves and lavender perfumed handkerchiefs, gifts from those who could ill afford it, yet a tangible comfort in knowing prayers are said for my safety and wellbeing.

The final farewell do was the huge Youth Rally held in a marquee on an open field, attended by over two hundred young people from as far afield as Malmesbury and Stellenbosch. That was a gathering that I will never forget, for it turned out to be the most memorable, and, given all that I had experienced in the preceding six months, perhaps the most fitting of my several farewells.

While we were in the marquee, singing and praising God, others in the community were marching in the streets, protesting against the brutal actions of the police who were rounding up young children and locking them up in prison for indefinite periods of time, quite often without the parents being aware of what had happened, or where their children were. In between the playing of guitars and the beating of drums, from time to time we could hear gunshots and shouting coming from outside in the street.

Just as I was about to make my farewell speech standing at the lectern, the canvas flap at the back of the marquee was thrown open and a young man of about nineteen or twenty years of age burst into the tent. He looked around at us, all clutching our hymn sheets, and then stared straight at me. Tears rolling down his cheeks, he said, "You Christians singing about Jesus, Jesus, all the time! I tell you what – Jesus has just been shot in the street!"

Those words pierced my heart and remain etched in my memory for ever. It was another moment of conviction that confirmed for me the kind of person I had to be. I knew that whatever happened, wherever I was, I could never just preach, and sing and pray; I had to act for justice, doing anything I could to make sure that people could have fullness of life.

And I did something that day. Even though I knew that I would soon be leaving, I took that young man home with me to live with my family. It seems strange to me now that, even though we lived in a small house with only 3 bedrooms (for eleven children, two parents and a grandparent) there always seemed to be enough space to squeeze just one more person in!

We discovered that for the young man I took home after my final farewell service, home had been an old broken-down bus, with no windows and no doors. The wheels of the bus didn't go round and round as in the children's nursery song, because there were no wheels left, they had all been taken off by someone looking for a way to make a quick buck! He lived in this contraption of rust and iron with his older brother. Their mother died of AIDS and he had no idea who his father was. My family and I were surprised that a person didn't know their father. In our family everyone knows about everybody else both in the family and in our immediate community. My mother, before she married my father, was teaching in the local primary school and my grandmother was known as the local midwife. We knew quite a bit about our local community!

Right to the very end of my time in South Africa, joy and pain, celebration and sorrow, kept on being woven together.

No one could say that I wasn't given a 'proper' send-off. I was well and truly prepared for my journey to 'the Queen's country', to give it my Aunt Stella's favourite name. She came to see me off and she handed me a white handkerchief embroidered with little purple daisies soaked in Yardley's Lavender Cologne. "Just in case you feel faint on the plane, Jenni; press this to your nose and inhale deeply" she instructed me as she pushed said hankie into my hand.

* * *

We were on our way to Cape Town international airport. My two new suitcases were packed and had been carried out to the car by two of my brothers. My father was waiting patiently in the car. My mother, who had been rummaging through her selection of hats, looking for one suitable to wear to the airport, finally emerged wearing a floral tea-cosy with a green feather perilously dangling over her left ear. She handed me the big Bible. "Here, you must have this. Put it in your hand luggage. It's tradition for the eldest to have the family Bible!" I left the Bible on the hallway table. There was excitement in the air, as my family processed to the waiting cars and the neighbours watched from their front gates. Some leaned out of their windows, waving, smiling, calling out to me: "Don't forget us; send a post card. God be with you. Send me a photo of the Queen!" I do not now remember how I felt, or what went through my mind. I think I made myself go blank so as not to think, or start crying. I do remember saying under my breath: "Goodbye, house, I don't know when I'll see you again."

My Dad was driving, and my youngest brother sat in front with him. I sat squashed between my mother and two of my sisters in the back. In the end there was a procession of three cars and a *bakkie* (pick-up) that was carrying seven members of the morning choir from church. All these people taking me and my two suitcases to Cape Town International airport! It was perhaps just as well that I did not know what awaited us at the airport.

I felt quite unnerved when I arrived at the airport and saw that there was already gathered there a crowd of familiar, unexpected faces. Waiting for me in the departure lounge was my aunt in her wheelchair. My two colleagues from the South African Council of Churches were there, as was Glenda, the stripper who had shared a prison cell and communion with me. Also coming to see me off at the airport were women from the Domestic Workers Union, and two sex workers I had taught to read and write. Handing me a small book of daily psalms was the minister and his wife from our local Methodist Church.

I also noticed out of the corner of my eye two men in felt hats, wearing black suits; they were from the Special Branch Police, and trying to look as if they were not Special Branch Police. Young people who attended my father's ballroom dancing class handed me a parcel wrapped in pretty floral paper, which I later discovered contained a beautiful evening ball gown. The seven members from the church choir gave a rousing rendition of one of my favourite hymns, "God will take care of you" and had half the airport singing with them!

I want to describe this scene in such detail, because it gives a sense of who I am; this tradition and the diversity of this gathering reflects so much of what has shaped me.

But the most endearing memory is of what my father said, just before I boarded the plane: "*Bokkie* (sweetheart), whatever you do in that strange country, remember where you come from. Remember where you come from." They were strange words; and not the sort of thing that my father would usually say. Of course, I know where I come from. My Mum and Dad begat me, as the Bible says, but what he meant was much more than that biological fact. My Dad held me close and our tears mingled. He pushed a piece of handwritten paper in my hand. "Here, read this. Read it when you're alone."

Mark was there at the airport, of course. Saying goodbye to him was so painful! In the parting image I have of him, he is standing with his arm around my Dad's shoulder, both looking as if they would burst into tears any moment. Both looking at me with such love shining out of their eyes, I forced myself to smile gaily as I pretended that my own heart was not breaking at this parting.

Eventually I found myself up in the air, and the tears flowed easily. I vowed that as soon as I landed in England, I would write a long letter to Mark. In the meantime, I opened the letter that my father had put into my hand. I have read it many times since then. I have typed it out and keep it in a plastic sleeve. It is written in my mother tongue, Afrikaans, and tucked into my Afrikaans Bible:

"Remember you come from a great and proud people whose mouths are always wide with laughter and whose tears fall for every downtrodden soul. You come from a people who are not afraid to work, pick the grapes, bathe the children, cook the chicken, scrub the floors in the white people's homes. You come from a people who marched down the street demanding to be treated like a human being; you come from people who sang songs of freedom from behind prison bars, a people who can kick up the dust like swirling mist when they dance the samba in the sand; you come from great-great grandmama and grandpapa who carried stones and built a place of worship where you learnt to recite the psalms of King David. You come from a People who know God and worship him in

Angry Love

the church, in the fields, on the mountain top. Walk tall. Walk proud. Take courage from those who paved the way for you to follow. You will always be surrounded by a cloud of unseen witnesses who will cheer you on life's pathway. God be with you 'til we meet again. Your Dada xxxx."

I don't know if my father wrote it, or someone else, but I have drawn immense courage from those words. I have tried to memorise them; I have used them in talks and in sermons and they have become like guiding posts on the way.

Angry Love

PART TWO

NEW COUNTRY; NEW LIFE

Angry Love

Chapter 5
Alien and Accepted

Boarding the aircraft at Cape Town airport was my first experience of being on an aeroplane. I was slightly apprehensive, but not frightened. I felt sad leaving my family behind, but also excited at the thought of what was waiting ahead for me. The flight was smooth and we landed early the next morning at Heathrow airport in London.

As I came through customs and out of the big sliding doors, a sea of unfamiliar faces swam in front of me. I saw a lady in a blue suit with a big wide smile who held a placard in front of her which said 'Methodist Church of Great Britain', and I went up to her. She introduced herself as Susan Barr, and gave me a warm hug; I felt accepted immediately.

Susan was terrific. She journeyed with me from the airport into central London, and then took the train with me from London to Sheffield, and accompanied me right to the Urban Theology Unit in Abbeyfield Road. She made sure that I met the staff and stayed with me until it was time for the evening meal. I was now well and truly in 'the Queen's country'.

First Impressions

I soon discovered that it was an 'alien' country – or perhaps I should say, rather, that I was an alien in a different country. There were so many times when I heard myself saying in those first weeks and months: "But that's not how we do it at home!" Everything was strange and different; and home seemed so far away. I missed home so much.

The people at UTU couldn't have been more welcoming, but I struggled to come to terms with all the differences I was facing and all the adjustments that I was having to make all the time. I was speaking a language that was not my own, and struggled to adjust to the Yorkshire accent and dialect, which was completely different from the English I had heard spoken by the Whites at home; I lived among people who were from a different ethnic group and whose culture was different from mine. I was living in a house where I had to climb a flight of stairs before I could reach the front door, and inside there were more stairs, when I had always only known single level, street level, living.

I missed seeing the mountains from my open bedroom window in the mornings; seeing the blue sky and catching the scent of the sea. I missed the sound of dogs barking, of the cockerel crowing and the hens clucking in our back yard. I missed hearing my neighbour screaming at her children! I felt as if I was living amongst a people who were hiding themselves away, or maybe they were just minding their own business, as my mother would say. It was baffling for me that when I saw people in the street and instinctively wanted to greet them as I would 'at home', but these complete strangers showed no sign of having a similar intention, and averted their eyes before I could open my mouth!

What I remember most about those early days, was drinking endless cups of tea, whether at church or in someone's home. Tea, tea, tea everywhere; a cup of tea when coming from the shops; tea when you sit down to have a chat; tea for arriving, and tea before leaving; anytime was teatime! It was the culture.

Food was another learning experience. I found it so bland. I missed my mother's cooking, her spicy stews, and her delicious puddings. The food prepared by the cook at UTU was wholesome and plentiful. I was introduced to baked potatoes with different fillings, and to Yorkshire pudding (which I discovered had nothing to do with dessert). It took some time for me to get used to having both roast potatoes and mashed potatoes on my plate, alongside meat pie, carrots and peas. On Sundays we had a typical English roast; well, it was called a roast, but if it was chicken – this was thinly sliced into flat white pieces, and so I would always ask for the skin, which was the only bit that was brown and looked roasted! There were lovely crispy roast potatoes, parsnips and swede (which was a first for me) and thick gravy. This was followed by apple crumble with custard. From my first taste, apple, rhubarb, or any fruit crumble, became my favourite English dessert. I loved it. Still do.

One week after my arrival at UTU, water started coming through the ceiling of my bedroom, and a plumber was called in. He discovered that this was not just a leaking pipe in the roof space, but that there was more serious damage and I had to move out. Plans was made for me to stay with an elderly lady, Mrs Plant, who lived by herself just along the road from the College.

Mrs Plant was ninety-two years old, and her house was a beautiful 'Tudor Style' dwelling; it looks exactly like the pictures I saw in English magazines back home. This house was big and beautiful, soft dove grey carpeted in the downstairs rooms. All the bedroom carpets were pastel shades of pink and blue and cream. One of the large rooms on the second floor was called the music room in which stood a grand piano and a table strewn with music sheets! On Saturday evenings after dinner and on some Sunday afternoons, Mrs P will 'tinker' (as she calls it) on the piano and we will sing the hymns we both know and loved. The house had three floors and I was given the loft bedroom on the third floor. It had a large bay window from which I could see the extensive back gardens of the neighbouring houses; they seemed almost like allotments, with their dazzling displays of colourful flowers, fruit trees, and vegetable patches. Taking pride of place in my bedroom, was a huge four poster bed with a duck feather eiderdown, and each night I snuggled into its softness and cosy warmth.

Mrs Plant was a bird like old lady with bright, merry blue eyes, and snow-white hair that fell in soft fat curls round her face. She was so sweet and very welcoming, and we became firm friends very quickly. She baked the most delicious sponge cakes and fed me well. At night after dinner and the washing up, the two of us would sit in front of the real fire in her sitting room and we would talk about our families. (Every day, one of Mrs Plant's neighbours, who was slightly younger than her, would carry in wood from the shed and start the fire for us.)

In a quavering voice, Mrs Plant would tell me about her "Dear William", who had died soon after returning from the war, and how she had loved him and was never able to love anyone after him. I listened with fascination as she took me on a journey from her childhood, as the privileged daughter of the local doctor, through to her "Coming-Out Ball" at seventeen. It was another world to me, and if it wasn't for the many sepia photos she produced, I think I might have felt it was all a dream.

She always wanted to know everything about South Africa and my large family. She knew quite a bit about Africa in general; she was interested in the world around her and kept a lively conversation. I stayed with 'Auntie Vera', as she insisted I called her, for eight weeks and grew extremely fond of her. She had an 'olde worlde' charm and was impeccably dressed when I came down for breakfast in the mornings. Her favourite was a blue chiffon dress with white snowdrops, and she mostly wore her pearl ear rings and two strings of pearls round her neck. I grew to love her.

When Mark and I got married (more of that later), Mrs Plant's present to us was a set of bone handle knives and forks, made in Sheffield, which had belonged to her "Dear mother", and which I have kept to this day! She died peacefully in her sleep at the age of ninety-nine. At the funeral a mutual friend, Richard, told me that a week before her death, he took her to see John Wayne (whom she adored) in one of his cowboy films. When Richard asked her if she enjoyed all the shooting and the fighting in the movie, she replied, diplomatically: "Didn't the soldiers look dapper in their splendid uniforms?" Dear Mrs Plant and others like her, made my settling into this new country such a warm welcoming experience; I was an alien, but accepted.

The weather was, of course, a big challenge! It seemed in those early days that the sky was always grey; no glimpse of blue for days on end. That first winter, it snowed heavily, and although the whiteness of the world was like the Christmas card pictures I had seen, I did have some nasty falls in the snow. I learnt the hard way, and very quickly, how to balance myself and walk without falling on snow, either freshly fallen or frozen hard.

One other aspect of the life and culture in Sheffield came as a shock to me, a very pleasant one, I have to say. It did not take long for our neighbours to cheerfully wave their hands in greeting and call out, "All right, love?" when they spotted me at the front gate. At first, I was completely taken aback, because 'back home', where segregation was legal and racism was commonplace; and white people could be as abusive as they liked, I had been called many names *'kaffermeid'*, *'hotnot'*, or *'koelie'*, but no white person had ever called me "love". It might have been just an expression there in Sheffield, but it was nice. I even began to use this term myself!

The feeling of warmth and acceptance reached a new level one day when I had to travel by bus to somewhere that I did not know. When I boarded the bus, I asked the driver to let me know when the stop that I needed was approaching, and to my surprise, as my getting off point came near it was not just the driver, but several of my fellow passengers who called out in chorus, "Next stop is yours, love!"

I might have been an alien, but over the years, I received so much kindness and acceptance, sometimes in the most unexpected places and at the most unexpected times, that it helped to heal some of the bruises and pain that I suffered in the place I had known as home. My sense of 'home' was growing and changing.

New ways of seeing

Six members of the Course lived in a large house that UTU used for student accommodation: Jonah and Naboth from Zimbabwe, Olaf from Norway, David from Kent, Esme and myself from South Africa. Three other students joined us for lectures, commuting daily from different parts of Yorkshire. There were also in the house two long-term tenants, Gigi and John, who did not take part in the course, but John became almost like a brother to me.

Lectures were held in a large room and the nine of us from such diverse backgrounds and different countries became friends and teachers to one another. Olaf from Norway showed pictures of his family and handed each of us a Norwegian scarf; Jonah from Zimbabwe taught us a song in Shona; everyone shared life lessons that reinforced my belief that each one of us come into this life to learn, to unlearn, to receive, or to refuse.

Not only did I learn about other countries, I made a lot of new discoveries about the different religions in the world. John Vincent's central aim was to make us aware that we were all citizens of another country – the Kingdom of God. And in God's country, he contended, things were different from the usual way we know of life and living. I came to be, both in awe of, and drawn into the "upside-down kingdom" inaugurated by Jesus, where 'the first shall be last; the poor shall inherit the earth, not the rich; the lowly are exalted, etc. etc.

In these classes I made so many new discoveries in the Bible and gained new insight into the Gospels. I found my love for the Bible stories rekindled and enjoyed the stimulating discussions around exegesis, history and biblical texts, finding them immensely informative. Each semester we had to write a module on one aspect of theology as seen from the bottom up (as seen and perceived by those on the margins of society), and present it to the whole class. This always led to amazing, lively discussions. I thoroughly enjoyed it.

It was all so new and refreshing to me; I drank liberally from all the overflowing cups of education that were put before me. I was learning in the company of radical thinkers, and being introduced to worlds previously unknown to me. Having focused so much on looking at Scripture through the eyes of oppressed women, I now learned to do so from other perspectives and with a broader world vision. It was as if more and more windows were being opened in my already inquiring mind. But, as none of the teaching or discussions was in

Afrikaans, one of my first purchases was an English dictionary, to help me with my understanding and use of English!

There were opportunities for us to visit many of the historic Cathedrals and other places of interest as a group of international students. We willingly became the captive audience for many a guide at these places and I always made quite sure that I came away with as many colourful information brochures as my bag could hold. I was fascinated by English history and felt drawn to old castles and ancient churches. I found that there was always something new to see and to learn whenever I went to these places.

The course was flying by and I felt happy that I had been given this privilege. But I still missed my family tremendously and I wrote regularly to my parents. I also made sure that I put aside a part of the money I received from the Bursary for my own support, so that I could slip a pound or two into the letters I sent: I knew that a single pound could make a real difference to my Mum as she struggled to 'make ends meet' back at home.

Reunion

On the flight from Cape Town to London, I had promised myself that I would write to Mark as soon as I arrived in England. He was quicker off the mark than I was, and I received his first letter eleven days after I left South Africa. It had been opened and re-sealed with cellotape. And I knew that our letters were being intercepted and examined by the security police in South Africa. Even though I expected that to happen, it was still a scary feeling every time I begin to open a letter from home.

Our only other means of communicating was by telephone. We arranged to call, long distance, about once a week, and I would run to the red telephone box on the corner of Abbeyfield Road, armed with a handful of coins. We would have such intimate conversations, expressing our longing, our growing love for each other, our frustration at living on different continents, and also talk about the things I was learning on my course. Mark never wanted to be the first to say goodbye, so we cram in as much as we could before the final bleep indicated that we ran out of money on both sides of the ocean.

It was through these telephone conversations that I came to realise that some of the letters that Mark sent just did not arrive. Other letters arrived with sentences obscured by thick black lines, so that it was impossible to read what Mark had written. It felt sinister that our intimate conversations were being read by unseen strangers and many times I wondered who are these people? What kind of person can feel at peace with themselves if their 'job' demands that they invade another's privacy?

But in spite of that, Mark's letters were a lifeline; I lived for his letters. They were so tender and transparent and revealed a side of Mark that I had not seen fully in the eighteen months that we had known each other before I left for England. In these letters he does not shy away from showing his vulnerability; there was a deep honesty in his writing, and reading his letters, I had no doubt that he was so much in love with me. I have kept some of those letters partly, I think, because I wanted my grandchildren to learn one of life's big lessons from them, which is, that we are all equal in our humanity and in our frailty, and that what matters is not the colour of one's skin, but who we are as persons.

I knew that Mark wanted desperately to join me in England, but there were so many barriers in the way, it seemed that this was not likely to happen: he had no passport, and no money for the flight; the authorities in South Africa were on the lookout for him, because of his refusal to do military service and his involvement in 'subversive activities'. But as with so much else in our strange relationship, things changed suddenly and dramatically.

* * *

It was Easter 1980, and John, who had become like a brother to me, invited me to Peckwood, a Retreat Centre in the heart of the Derbyshire countryside for the Easter weekend. On the Easter Monday, we received a call from Gigi, one of the tenants who lived in the student house at UTU, saying that a young man, named Mark, had knocked on the door and asked for me.

It's a cliché, but it's true in this case that "You could have knocked me over with a feather!" My body went all numb and my heart started beating so loud I could hear and feel it against my chest. I was flabbergasted. He hadn't said anything in our last conversation! How did he get to England? What had happened? Well, I had to keep all my questions for later.

John and his friend Nick, bundled me into the pickup truck and Nick drove like a maniac through the quiet Yorkshire roads. We arrived in Pittsmoor around one o clock that Easter Monday afternoon. My heart lurched and thumped and almost burst when I saw my beloved. He looked exhausted, but his smile was radiant and it reached his eyes. They were shining as he looked at me. He opened his arms and engulfed me in the tightest hug ever! We both had tears streaming down our faces and just held on to one another. Oh my God, oh dear Lord, what a sweet reunion that was; what a beautiful time to be alive.

Mark was wearing his charity shop blue RAF (magic) coat, and his hair was a mass of golden curls tumbling down to his shoulders. He looked gorgeous and the looks he gave me were just so full of pure love. My sister says ours was a real romantic love story where the man cross oceans to be with the woman he loves.

I had to report to Margaret Mackey, the college secretary that my fiancé had arrived, and requested permission for him to use the visitors' room. She said that she could see no problem with that as there were no bookings for that month. And so, for the last three months of the academic year, Mark joined me on the Training Course and took fully part in all aspects of the Course.

John Vincent and the other tutors were very interested in our situation and encouraged Mark to tell the story of his perilous journey to England. The first hurdle for Mark to overcome had been his not having any legal travel documents. Because he had refused to do what was expected of all white males of his age, namely, to join up with the South African Defence Force, he had no "legal registration" anywhere, except his ID Document, which all South Africans have to carry. Mark had therefore approached comrades in the ANC offices in Lusaka to help him with a travel document. The underground liberation movement provided him with a 'passable' passport, with an authentic photo, and he also was given a United Nations travel document, which was valid for one year only.

As he talked, at times with tears in his eyes, my beloved shared haltingly how he went to say good bye to my youngest sister Patti at the high school she attended. He waited for her outside the school gates and as they walked home together, he told her that he was planning to leave the country to join me in England. He asked her not to say a word to anyone, but to wait for three days, by which time he would be across the border into Botswana, and then tell the family. He then also gave her a letter to post to his parents.

He left Cape Town quietly. With no words of farewell, no prayers being said for travelling mercies, no family or friends to see him off. He had only one thing in his mind and that was to get to me as soon as possible. Like most fugitives, he left under cover of darkness; he had only his back pack and a small pocket Bible.

Between South Africa and Botswana, there was a fence that was electrified and guarded, which Mark had to cross. He had waited until two o'clock in the morning before he started walking along the fence and found a small section where he could crawl underneath it to the other side. Once in Botswana, he linked up with a priest from the Catholic Church, John Osmers, an ANC supporter, who offered him place to stay while waiting for word from the ANC in Lusaka.

It was arranged that for part of his journey, Mark was to travel on a truck that was carrying farm produce to Lusaka. Mark was dressed in the conventional blue farm workers overalls; he was accompanied by three farm workers who were similarly dressed. On arriving in Lusaka Mark made his way to the ANC offices and was given food and accommodation by the comrades in exile there.

He lived with the comrades there for three weeks, sat at their feet and learnt more of the internal structures and activities of the underground movement. They were not at all eager for him to leave, as they could see that as a white man he would have been able to move around more freely than any of the black comrades could, and he would have been a great asset to the Movement, acting as a courier between those active on the ground and those working underground.

However, Mark told them about me, and our longing to be together. They must have understood in the end, because Mark brought with him a card that was signed with the names of comrades I did not even know. It made me feel good inside, and it gave me a sense of our tumultuous relationship being part of something deeper and bigger. And that there are a larger group of supportive people around us, cheering us on, validating our relationship.

* * *

The week after his unexpected arrival, Mark was insistent that the first thing we should do was to go to London, to let 'our people' know that we are here, and that, should the need ever arise, we were available to the Movement. We hitch-hiked from Sheffield to London, and back, and what an experience that was! I could write a book about the amazing, the weird, and the funny characters we met as we travel in vehicles ranging from ... lorries, people carriers, or a lone driver in a sports GM. There were numerous times when I was full of uncertainty and fear, and I would never have done it if Mark wasn't beside me. I couldn't help wondering what people made of us, a tall white man and a short brown woman standing beside each other with thumbs held out hopefully. In the following months, this was to become our standard mode of long-distance travel, as we didn't have the money to travel by any other means. These journeys certainly provided us with hilarious material for lively late-night conversations with our housemates whenever we came back to Sheffield. On this particular day, we set off armed with a map of London and we eventually found our way to Penton Street, where the ANC headquarters in London were located. It was immediately as if we had walked into the bosom of the family; we were treated like children whose return home had been long waited for. Chief in charge, comrade Ruth Mompati, opened her arms and held me like my mother would, in a great warm welcome; Eleanor Khanyile, George Johannes and Lindiwe Poswa formed a little circle around us and hung onto our lips for morsels from home. We spent a pleasant morning, not without a few tears been shed – at home away from home.

Mark was given a bag full of literature, and an ANC t-shirt, and comrade Ruth whispered to me: "I know what it's like coming to this country in your circumstances. You will need this", as she discreetly pushed an envelope into my hand. Such sensitive kindness. Just as we were about to leave, as we were saying goodbye at the door of the offices, a distinguished looking man in a dark grey suit climbed out of a London cab that pulled up outside the door. As he looked up, he waved and I saw that it was Oliver Tambo, one of the stalwarts of our struggle! I recognised his face from the photos I had seen. I couldn't believe my eyes; I had goose bumps on my arms and was completely overwhelmed with emotion.

He was an impressive man and he exuded charisma and warmth. He ushered us back through the door saying he'd like to make our acquaintance. *Joh!* I thought, I must be dreaming, as he asked for tea and cake to be brought into his little office and waved Mark and myself onto a two-seater, and lowered himself into a cosy armchair. There I was with in the same room with OR! I touched his hand, but beyond that I could only smile and nod and nothing else. I was tongue tied and gave my full attention to eating cake and drinking tea while he and Mark went into a rather serious conversation. Most of which escapes me now – as it did then! But when we finally left that afternoon, it was with a firm commitment to come to London regularly so that we could work within the ANC structures for the liberation of our people and country.

* * *

Angry Love

After our visit to the ANC offices, and about fourteen days after Mark's arrival, two British Immigration Officials arrived on doorstep of UTU. They said that the Immigration Department had discovered that Mark used a falsified travel document to enter Britain and that he would therefore have to be deported and that they had come to carry out the deportation.

The immigration officers were invited to come into the house, and after a long discussion, John Vincent persuaded the officers to allow Mark one more day at UTU, and that he, John, would be held personally responsible if Mark did not turn up at the airport the following day to be deported back to Lusaka. Well, the whole of Abbeyfield Road, the students at UTU, and the local church community spent that night in prayer with us, hoping that there would be some dramatic intervention, but, disappointingly, as is so often the case, that didn't happen then. The atmosphere around the college was like someone had died, and our hearts were heavy with trepidation.

The following morning Mark and myself were accompanied to Heathrow Airport by Roy Crowder, on behalf of UTU; Brian Brown, our Minister-Friend; and Maureen, a lawyer from UKIAS (United Kingdom Immigration and Asylum Seekers). There we were met by the officers who had come to UTU and, holding out hand chains, they approached Mark. Brian Brown intervened quietly but firmly, asking why hand chains were necessary as Mark was not a criminal, and pointing out that he had voluntarily come to the airport to be deported. The officers accepted the point in a quite friendly manner and did not press for the handcuffing. We found an empty table to sit down.

Maureen told Mark that he should not worry about anything (!); she pointed out that it was important to comply with the British Immigration Rules, and that he should admit to having entered the country using a false passport. She ended by assuring him that she would be working non-stop to get him returned to the UK as soon as possible. When you're in that kind of situation where you feel helpless, you just let go and let those who know what they're doing, take control of the situation. And so, we just let ourselves be held (mentally, spiritually) by the dear friends surrounding us.

Mark bought a Danish pastry, and as we sat, each with a cup of coffee or tea, we passed the pastry around and said to one another, "The body of Christ given for you." Another holy moment. Mark and I were both crying openly, and our friends encircling us looked grave as we held hands and Brian offered a prayer for guidance and help. The most heart-breaking memory of that day for me, was to see Mark walking between the two officers, heading towards the departure lounge. Just before going through the doors, he turned around, smiled that enigmatic smile, waved and was gone. And my heart flew out of me and went with him.

Afterwards I went with Brian and Maureen straight to the UKIAS offices in central London, where I had to fill in numerous forms and answer detailed questions about the reasons why Mark and I were seeking political asylum in Britain. Things really got moving then, and it began to seem that, on our behalf, God was really working hard – through people.

Maureen took steps straightaway to get Mark returned to the UK as soon as possible. She lodged the necessary papers with the Courts and the Immigration Service, and contacted a member of the Board of Amnesty International with information about Mark's case. In the meantime, the Border police in Lusaka were far from happy about the presence of a white South African among the all-black detainees held in custody on their patch; they wanted Mark out of their country as soon as possible. This worked in our favour, and combined with Maureen's hard work in her legal circles, Mark was returned to Britain seven days after he left. What a day of rejoicing that was, the students at UTU hang banners of welcome in front of the college and a bunch of balloons at the entrance. The neighbours in the street came out with drinks and cakes and we gave thanks to God, played music and danced on the lawn in front of the college for all the world to see.

Maureen urged strongly that we should try to get married as soon as possible, as it would simplify the paperwork and strengthen our case if we were applying for refugee status as husband and wife, rather than as two independent people. Well, as this was now the end of April, we had exactly three months in which to plan a wedding!

A wedding with a difference

The wedding day, 7 August 1981, dawned quietly; there were blue skies, but a cold wind was blowing. It was an eclectic mix of people that gathered in Pittsmoor Methodist Church to witness us become husband and wife. There was the group of international students from Urban Theology Unit; Father John Osmers, whose arm had been blown off by a parcel bomb (sent by the apartheid security forces), that exploded as he was opening the package; there were several residents from Abbeyfield Road; the builders who were working on a block of flats across the road from the church (still wearing their work clothes and hard hats); the two ladies from the local Oxfam shop, where I had become a regular customer; ten people from the Ashram Community; four friends who flew in from Zimbabwe; the Labour Councillor for our particular Ward; and the Lord Mayor of Sheffield, who lived in the house next to Mrs Plant's, where I had stayed for eight weeks.

I thought that Mark looked gorgeous in his wedding outfit: dark red, flared, velvet pants and a white cotton mandarin collar shirt, with brown sandals on his feet. I wore a cheese cloth top and a skirt with lots of lacy frills (bought cheaply from the market in Portobello Road in London, during one of the day trips to the ANC office). On my head I wore a crown of white and yellow daisies, which Mark and David had picked fresh from the fields very early that morning. On my feet were the cream-coloured wooden clogs that my sister Philly had bought me as a going away present when I left South Africa.

It was a joyous occasion and it was clear that everyone, I mean everyone, was there to pour their good wishes over us. There must have been over a hundred people there altogether, and it was hard to envisage a more diverse gathering. It was so thrilling to realise that they were all there for Mark and for me. Many of the guests hugged and held us and expressed their admiration saying that we are brave and our love will conquer all. Almost everyone offered their support whenever we need it. It was all so moving and loving and kind. I was floating on a pink cloud of happiness and couldn't believe that this was MY wedding day. Something was missing though, I was conscious of our parents and our siblings, faraway in South Africa, who could not be with us, but who would be thinking of us and rooting for us on this special day. I was sure that they would be supporting us with their love and prayers, but that there would also almost certainly be concerns and doubts in their minds, because of the unusual nature of the marriage I was entering into. I had no doubts whatsoever.

The Minister who married us was a mutual friend, Brian Brown, a white Methodist Minister, who eight years earlier had been escorted out of South Africa by Special Branch men, and was told never to return. I met Brian Brown at one of the Christian Institute meetings. It felt right that he should lead the service and preach at this most significant event in our lives. My dear friend Theo Kotze, who lived in England at the time, was too ill to be with me, but we spoke on the telephone early that morning.

I decided that I would not come into church to the traditional strains of 'Here comes the bride', because this was our day, not just mine. So, Mark and I held on to each other as we walked down the aisle together. At our entrance, our friend, David played "Jesu joy of man's desire" on his trumpet accompanied by the church organist.

The marriage service was deeply moving, especially when the time came for Mark to make his vows. I can see him now. There were tears in his eyes, those blue eyes shining so bright, I drowned in them. His face was alight as if with some inner glow. He looked me full in the face and held my gaze with such tenderness I started to cry. He held my hands tightly, and in that deep, clear voice, he said:

> "Jen, I have loved you for a long time. We have been through so much together and my love grew all the stronger the more I got to know you. I have no worldly possessions to give you. All I have is my love for you – I love you with every fibre of my being. I thank God for you and for bringing us together.
>
> I marry you today and will marry you every day hereafter, because every day I will want to honour you, love you, hold you, share with you, listen to you. I want to lay myself before you and give you my vulnerability. So many times you could've walked away from this relationship. At times it was hard for both of us. There were many people who was sceptical about us, of what we stand for. Many more made fun of us and treated our being together as a freak show. But there are many – and some are here today – who prayed for us and rejoiced in our discovery of each other.
>
> We have been through tough times, and perhaps will go through some even tougher times in the future. But I want you to know that I shall be there with you, together we will make our marriage work. Together we will hold each other up and together we will bring about a different and more caring society. You are all I ever wanted. I marvel at your warmth, and the care you have shown me. No-one has ever cared for me the way you do, Jen. I was surprised, and continue to be surprised, that you ever cared for me!
>
> I have no fear of the future, because you are in it with me and I shall pray every day that I will make you happy. God has given us to each other to have and to hold forever. I love you deeply, Jen, I always will and so I give you my trust.

Angry Love

Ja, ja", he concluded, nodding his head up and down in affirmation.

I could hear some guests blowing their noses, and a few men coughing, and there was a long silence when Mark finished making his promises to me. It took Brian, the Minister, a while before he could continue with the rest of the service. For my part, I told Mark that I would always love him; not always with lust or with eros love, but with humaneness. He just looked at me with that enigmatic smile and said, 'Oh, Jen, you....,' and shook his head.

When we had made our vows to each other, we made one further declaration; standing before that diverse congregation of friends and supporters we said together:

> "We, Mark and Jenni, have at this moment in time, no country to call our own since we dare not return to South Africa for fear of persecution. We have, as yet, received no confirmation of our status in THIS country. We have, as yet, no home to call our own. But today we want to commit ourselves to live in such a way that wherever HOME will be for us, we will make space to give refuge for stranger and friend who find themselves in similar position as ours. God being our helper".

(It is a commitment that was sometimes to prove costly, but it is one that we have never regretted, and over the years, because of that vow we made, and the circumstances that gave rise to it, I have made sure that wherever I was, and whatever my situation, the home I had was always a hub where South Africans, in particular, could meet and eat.)

After the service, it was a joy to see our guests in all their diversity mingling freely with one another. There was so much generosity shown to us that day: all the refreshments were provided by friends who came laden with huge platters of food and cakes and, dressed in their finery, cheerfully carried them into the church hall where the reception was to be held. There was a live band that always play at the Barn Dance that the church held each year, and they kept our guests dancing until midnight. It was a day that felt miraculous and full of hope; a day that I will never forget. On Mark's face, there was a huge, constant smile. For me there was certainly deep happiness, but also a bit of discomfort at the intensity of it all, some embarrassment at being the centre of so much attention, and more than a tinge of regret that none of my five sisters was able to be with me on this special day. How they would've revelled in the attention, how they would've danced with no inhibitions!

When we opened the wedding presents, we found that many of our guests had thoughtfully brought useful gifts such as sheets and china – and, as already mentioned, the cherished cutlery set from Mrs Plant. There was a cheque for £500 (a huge amount in those days and it would still be seen as extremely generous even now) from Al Green, the Labour Councillor for our Ward and I had to swallow hard later, when Mark took this cheque, which had been given for us to start our new life together, and handed it to the ANC, to be used, he said, for the needs of our comrades who lived in camps in the countries bordering South Africa, and who sacrificed their lives for the freedom of our people. I was not happy, I would've given half to the ANC and kept half for us. After all, we had nothing really, and it was our wedding gift! But that's how Mark was...

A fellow student, Jean, had offered us the chance to stay at her house in Dumfries while she was away, and so after the wedding, we went there for two weeks. It was there, in the Scottish country side, that Mark taught me to ride a bike, though it was so unnerving for me when we were met on the country lanes by cows returning to their fields after being milked! Every time this happened, which it seemed to almost every day, I climbed off the bike and pushed it into the mud and ditches to get away as far as I could from what seemed to me such cross-looking cows descending upon me en masse.

* * *

Mark and I had such fun together and laughed a lot. He was young, loving and giving, and we were deeply in love. We discovered more and more about each other. We realised that alongside our now being husband and wife, we were first and foremost good friends who

Angry Love

shared a common love for books, classical music and South African jokes! We took long walks in the green, green Scottish Highlands, had picnics next to gurgling streams and we baked bread in Jean's kitchen. There were no cell phones in those days, and the television didn't always work so we read and sang hymns, and freedom songs and wrote long letters to our families. We returned to Sheffield refreshed, and needed to be, as we faced the challenge and uncertainty of the year ahead.

Transition

Mark and I realised that it was out of the question for us to return to South Africa when my one-year course at UTU ended. The situation at home was becoming critical politically. The apartheid regime was becoming ever more brutal, introducing more draconian laws and banning more and more organisations and prominent people. Our lives would be in danger, as we were known to the Security Police through the infamous informer network operating both nationally and inter-nationally. Or we could be prosecuted under the 'Immorality Act', for being 'illegally married' according to South African law. Several of our friends were taken into prison, were released after a time without any charge brought against them. Many of them ended up in Canada, GDR. We realised the only option was for us to find a way of remaining in England.

But that wouldn't be easy. Mark had no official documents, except the piece of paper from the United Nations which allowed him entry into Britain for a year. After the incident of his deportation and return, we both were issued with green cards from the British Immigration services. This booklet certified that we are legally allowed to remain in the South Yorkshire area, but that privilege had to be validated every fourteen days, with a stamp in the book from the local police constabulary. It was to take a total of eight long years of waiting for answers from the Home Office, before we were eventually given 'leave to remain in the UK unconditionally'.

As my year at UTU was drawing to a close, John Vincent decided that the best course of action was for me to be continued as a student registered with UTU for a further year, and for Mark also to be enrolled as a student of UTU. After our wedding we moved out of the house on Abbeyfield Road and into another house owned by the circuit. Miraculously, and by God's grace, ways were found to cover the costs of our studying and our accommodation. We lived in Sheffield for less than a year when another door was opened for us in a strange way.

Chapter 6
Called to Serve

During my 'extension year' at the Urban Theology Unit in Sheffield, I was invited to be the guest speaker at a conference arranged by a group within the Methodist Church called 'Methodists for World Mission'. The conference was to be held at Swanwick, Derbyshire and when I asked if Mark could come with me, the organisers readily agreed. They were clearly thrilled to have Mark there, and gave him the opportunity to speak about the danger and difficulty of his leaving South Africa.

That weekend changed our lives. We met so many people who wanted to hear, not only Mark's story, but our shared story, and we received several invitations to speak in various Methodist churches and to different organisations.

One of the organisers of the Swanwick conference, Rachel Stephens, sat with us for a very long time. When she heard that we would shortly be leaving UTU, and that we would have nowhere to live after that, she became very excited and said that we were exactly what her church community in Notting Hill was looking for, and asked if we would consider moving to London? The church had just advertised a post which was for a woman who would become part of the Team Ministry at Notting Hill. Accommodation would be provided in a small, one bedroom flat that was owned by the Church. Rachel urged me to apply and said that she would write a letter in support of my application.

That night Mark and I talked through what the future looked like for us. We had no money, no home, no family, and no jobs. Rachel's offer came like an answer to our prayers! We decided that I should apply for the post – and so began yet another journey into the unknown, a journey that brought with it life changing opportunities and challenges.

We moved to London, and I began working as part of the leadership team in the Church, and Mark started his work for the South African Congress of Trade Unions, SACTU. Mark dedicated his time, his labour, his skills, his heart and soul to this work, which he saw as his vocation.

Being in Community

When the community in Notting Hill heard that we were political refugees from South Africa, people came with open, smiling faces. Neighbours, church members and friends brought cutlery, crockery, blankets and cooking pots I remember one of them, Rachel, brought two boxes filled with plates, cups and dishes. After removing from the collection only two cups, two plates and two dishes, Mark and I returned the rest of the things to Rachel the following day. We believed that two of each would be sufficient for our use and that we did not need over and above that; we did not want to accumulate things, or have too many possessions. We felt that as our status is hanging in limbo, and if we are refused refugee status here in the UK, we'll have to move somewhere else and too much stuff is going to be a hindrance. Also, for Mark it was a lifestyle principle (and a kingdom prerogative), to travel lightly through life.

Rachel taught me a lesson I have never forgotten. She said: "Jenni you must learn to accept when people want to bless you. Learn to receive a gift and appreciate the many ways care for you is being expressed. I suggest that you keep all these things that were given to you. You will need it when visitors come. How can I drink tea with you if you have only two cups; or how can you offer me a plate of food if you have only two plates!" I learned that sacred and gracious lesson, and from then on, I welcomed and accepted with a grateful heart the things people in their kindness offered me.

I came to see that people genuinely cared about our perilous political situation and were deeply concerned about the turbulent political climate we fled from. Those were the days when 'strangers' would come and stock our cupboards with food. Others came and prayed with us, and filled our small flat with love and songs and gave us pictures to hang on the walls. There were many others who picked us up in their cars, or walked with us to the local Methodist Church, where we found a spiritual home. In this church fellowship we experienced koinonia in a community of young and old, black and white, rich and poor, discovering what it means to be disciples of Jesus.

There was Mrs Holder who insisted that we have Sunday lunch with her family. And what a lunch! The table groaned under large dishes of goat curry, rice and peas, macaroni cheese, and a variety of vegetables. I remember how we used to walk home slowly with bellies too full to hurry, as we reach our place we threw ourselves onto the bed and slept for most of the rest of the afternoon. I remember 'well off' young couple who lived in the flat below us and who gave us their radio, cooking pots, warm jumpers and a winter coat before they emigrated to Canada. I remember Mrs Hashni from Pakistan who lived opposite us, who took me round the market, cooked delicious *saag aloo* (a spinach and potato dish), showed me where the doctor's surgery was and helped me to register, and taught me how to cook basmati rice.

The Methodist Church in Notting Hill became our extended family. We quite quickly became part of this vibrant, diverse congregation and our spirit soared as we sang the old familiar hymns, and studied the scriptures together in the weekly Bible studies, bringing insights from our particular contexts.

Church bazaars were a sight to behold, with tables groaning under the weight of *ackee* and salt fish, and jerk chicken from Jamaica; buns and scones from the English ladies; curry, *samoosas* and *chaat* from the Indian ladies – all proudly showing off their cooking and baking skills, and sharing the products of their labour with everyone.

Strangers from the Caribbean, Africa, Pakistan and Ireland became friends and confidants. As the years passed, we became one another's keepers; we looked out for one another. We helped out where we could; we walked together to church and waited together at the school gates for our children. We greeted each other in the local supermarket like long lost family!

Slowly, steadily, this strange place became home, and the strange people became my people for they were strangers no longer; they became my friends who had a place in my heart and to whom my home would always be open.

Learning and growing

An opportunity was offered for me to go further with my studies and training. In September 1981, I began a course in Cross Cultural Communications, specially tailored to my particular needs; it involved me spending part of my time at the Selly Oak Colleges in Birmingham, and taking the final part at Horsforth College in Leeds.

In the Selly Oak part of the course, I was the only female student alongside seven men from different parts of the world: India, Africa and the Philippines. My knowledge of the wider world increased vastly in a very short time. I enjoyed this further period of studying as a mature student. I devoured

books on Theology and English society in almost equal measure!
We did 'mock' radio interviews, wrote scripts for radio, and I
lost some of my Cape Town accent as I learnt how to speak to
a listening radio audience.

The Selly Oak Colleges was a Federation of colleges that were
geographically close to each other in the south of Birmingham.
I lived in one of those colleges called Woodbrook, which was
owned and run by the Quakers, and when I was not attending
a Methodist Church, I enjoyed the silence of the Quaker
worship. It was at Woodbrook where I was drawn to classical
music, the Principal organised for live classical music every

Fellow students: International Centre for Cross Cultural
Communications at Selly Oak Colleges, Birmingham.

Sunday evening during the summer months. Even though I
got confused and could never remember who composed which
piece of music, I began to enjoy the ebb and flow of concertos
by famous composers like Bach, Mozart and Carl Jenkins. And
as I sat there in an audience of mainly elderly white folk, I
smiled to myself as I remember one of my telephone calls home
to my parents and my sister (who was still at school) asking
me if that kind of music don't put me to sleep!

Angry Love

The students at the Selly Oak colleges were usually 'mature' and came from all over the world; some had family members with them. There were social events arranged for anyone who was part of the colleges, including family members. Through these events I made friends with women from Bolivia and learnt about their husbands who worked in the mines, about their struggles and exploitation by big multi-nationals; I met women from Northern Ireland who taught me Irish dancing! Beyond the Colleges, Birmingham had much to offer for my leisure time: the museum and art galleries, the canal with its repaired walkways, and a bustling market in the Bullring.

I made life-long friends and discovered patient mentors among this group of pilgrims who shared and ran this Course of study for international students. I enjoyed stimulating, informative conversations in the lecture rooms, and appreciated the time and attention my tutors at Selly Oak gave me. Every day my prayers were filled with gratitude for Mark's safe arrival, and that at last we're together, and for the learning opportunities offered to me in the salubrious surroundings of the Selly Oak Colleges. We had our own tennis courts; there was a Japanese garden with small bonsai trees; a pond which was the home of a family of white swans; oak and elm trees border the green landscape surrounding the college and birdsong filtered through the open windows into our lecture rooms. It was hard to imagine anything that could be further removed in tone and spirit from the streets of Cape Town and the painful violent (laws) struggle for the liberation of my homeland.

Before going to bed each night, I would take out my old Methodist hymn book and sing to myself in my room the familiar words of one or more of the hymns that is so much a part of my spiritual formation. The one that I returned to again and again was one that carried me through many of the most difficult periods of my life, one that stayed with me through moving from place to place, new friendships, new exposures, and gave me the assurance that God would accompany Mark and myself as we continued our journey together:

Be not dismayed; whate'er betide, God will take care of you;
Beneath his wings of love abide, God will take care of you.
God will take care of you, through every day, for all the way,
He will take care of you; God will take care of you.

Kingdom Lessons

After completing my course at Selly Oak, I continued to work for the church in Notting Hill three days each week for the next few years. For me this was a time of enjoyment and challenge and continued growth. I learned many 'kingdom lessons' while in Notting Hill, and some of them were so hard to grasp, I'm not sure, even now, that I understand them fully, but some incidents stand out above others, like the one in 1984 when Rev Mark Stephenson, a white minister who served the Methodist Church in the Cape of Good Hope District, brought a 'racially mixed' delegation of young people from the Methodist Youth Clubs in South Africa to England, which was in itself a radical thing to do at that time. Notting Hill was chosen as one of the stop-over places on their trip because of its significance in the history of Black people in Britain and because Mark Stephenson and I know each other from back home.

My husband Mark and I made arrangements for an open forum to be held between the visitors and Black members of our church. I think we called it 'South meets West', or something like that. The aims were (a) to share ideas and stories about the riots in SA and the riots in Notting Hill in the 1970s; (b) for the church in Notting Hill to learn how they could be in solidarity more intentionally with people struggling in South Africa; (c) to see whether and if so, how a reciprocal trip could be made from England to South Africa. It seemed a promising and potentially fruitful list of aims and there was subdued excitement in the air as the hosts welcomed their South African guests.

However, there was a problem before we could even begin the evening's event. The group from Notting Hill said that they would not speak unless the white members of the South African group left the room! It fell to me to convey this ultimatum to the Reverend Mark. Needless to say, he was upset and tried, as he saw it, to defuse the situation by falling on his knees in front of the Notting Hill people and begging their forgiveness on behalf of the white people in South Africa. My mouth would not close, as I stared at Mark with a mixture of pride and embarrassment. Oh, my goodness, what next?

In a kindly, but resolute manner, the spokesperson for the Notting Hill group said that they accepted his personal apology, and that he would be welcome to re-join the group for tea when the discussions were concluded, but the main business, 'this thing' as they termed it, was best done solely between those who were part of the oppressed, on both sides of the ocean.

Mark Stephenson was in tears as I escorted him and two of the young people from his group to our flat, which was not far away from the Church. Mark was still very emotional when we arrived there, but said to me that he could understand how the Notting Hill members saw the racial dynamics: he recognised that the Methodist Church in Notting Hill, having for years shown solidarity with the black people in South Africa against white supremacy, would then see the ordeal of baring their souls in front of white South Africans, as going against what they stood for. He did not return to the church for tea that evening, but that conversation cemented our friendship, and it has remained firm to this day.

The Notting Hill Carnival has become known around the world and the ANC was given the opportunity to enter a float for the Carnival Parade in August 1984. That weekend our small flat was completely taken over and overwhelmed by ANC comrades and young supporters, who quickly made themselves at home. We all spent several hours working happily together preparing the decorations for the float, using the ANC colours of black, gold and green; and then spent almost as much time laughing and eating right into the early hours of the morning. They had each brought a sleeping bag, and when the time came for them to settle down for the night, somehow, they each managed to find in that tiny flat, a corner where they could snatch a few hours of sleep. It was an exhilarating experience; for me a taste of the Kingdom. Among the group were the poet Wally Serote, and Dali Tambo, the son of Oliver Tambo.

* * *

It was in that same year, that Cedric Mayson, Barney Pityana, a young Rabbi named Selwin with myself and others, formed the ANC Religious Committee (UK). Notting Hill Methodist Church provided without charge, a room where the group could meet. The Mile End Methodist Church on the eastern side of London also allowed us, as a gesture of solidarity, to use their premises for our quarterly meetings. I felt very small and humble as I sat at the feet of these religious, politically conscious cadres. Once or twice Frene Ginwala joined our discussions – oh she was a formidable lady, very clever and very warm towards me.

With Dr Frene Ginwala (left on picture), Speaker of the National Assembly of South Africa from 1994 to 2004 and Chancellor of the University of KwaZulu Natal in 2004

With Dr Barney Pityana who, together with Steve Biko, founded South African Students' Organisation of the Black Consciousness Movement and became the Principal and Vice-Chancellor of the University of South Africa 2001-2010)

Speaking on behalf of SACTU at Centre for African & Oriental Studies, Covent Gardens, London.

Angry Love

Living in two worlds

Mark, in the meantime, immersed himself fully in the tumultuous life of the trade union movement. He ably represented SACTU, both nationally and internationally. He was, and continues to be, an idealist. He was committed to the freedom of the South African people. He believed in the people's right to be free, and he had a clear understanding of his own role in bringing about the necessary political change for the workers of South Africa. He sacrificed many long hours and days doing research, running workshops, meeting workers and comrades from all over the world. Mark breathed and lived "the struggle".

During this time a 'State of Emergency' was declared at home; there was the formation of the first National Congress of South African Trade Unions, (COSATU); the banning of several prominent figures and the organised clarion call from our people to 'make South Africa ungovernable', in which the 'underground' movement was allied to a mass movement on the ground. The work of the Movement intensified and Mark's role was pivotal and all consuming. He spent less and less time at home and more time in important meetings with comrades from home and supporters in the UK. His work in the trade union movement took him to Europe, Canada and the Soviet Union.

* * *

It was a demanding time for me also. Before leaving South Africa, I had become a 'Fully Accredited Local Preacher', that is a lay person who was seen by their own church community as having the gifts and graces to lead worship and to preach, and who had completed a course and examinations authorised by the wider church, to allow them to do so. After becoming a Local Preacher, I had continued to sense an urge to do more 'to work with God and change lives' and I had been accepted for training to become a 'Deaconess', the first Coloured woman to be accepted for that preparation in the Methodist Church of Southern Africa. My imprisonment and the events that followed meant that I was not able to even begin the course.

While working as part of the Team Ministry in Notting Hill, I had begun to sense a re-awakening of that earlier call, and when I shared this with Mark, he was bowled over, but also immediately and unreservedly supportive. That gave me the courage to talk with my colleagues in the team and a meeting of the Church Council followed. The Church Council listened, prayed with me, conferred, and gave their blessing to my beginning the long process of discernment and preparation that could lead to me start my training as a candidate for ministry in the Methodist Church.

Part of that preliminary preparation was to take various 'candidating exams' and I was studying for these. At the same time, I was continuing as a member of the Team Ministry in Notting Hill; volunteering at the SACTU offices; travelling around this country and wider afield to Ireland and countries in mainland Europe, raising awareness of the dire situation in South Africa and raising money to support the liberation movement.

Alongside all that Mark was involved in, I also did two days of voluntary work in the SACTU offices in Angel, Islington. The head of the offices at that time was Comrade Archie Sibeko (or ZZ, as he was usually called); my role was helping Comrade Eddie Ramsdale in the Finance Department.

There's no question that throughout our married life Mark and I spent a disproportionate amount of time (Mark even more so), working for our freedom; whatever social life we managed to have was usually in the context either of ANC Unit Meetings, or church functions! Alongside the official large annual fundraising of the ANC, we also did a lot of personal fundraising, with the support of our congregation in Notting Hill. We secured a market stall on the world-famous Portobello Road (Mark and I paid the rental for this out of our own pockets) and there we would sell bric-a-brac we had collected from our local church and other churches within our Circuit.

I always thank God for the ongoing support and prayers we received from the Methodist community. (Even on our wedding day, we asked for a collection be taken in the church so that we could send the money to the ANC camp in Tanzania, and our wedding guests gave very generously that day.)

* * *

It was while we were living in Notting Hill that our son, Themba, was born. His name means 'Hope' and he was a joy and blessing for Mark and myself, especially as I had suffered a miscarriage in the years before his birth. Themba's baptism was a moment of deep revelation for me. I saw, how despite fears and struggles and hindrances, life moves forward always; never backwards. It was while standing with my new-found family around the font in Notting Hill Church that this realisation dawned on me.

We were missing our families, we knew that the struggle was becoming more intense each day, and yet here we were celebrating new life, and doing what parents have done even from the times of the Old Testament, bringing our son to the House of the Lord, to be received and welcomed not into a random collection of people, but into the close-knit family in Notting Hill, representing the worldwide family of God. Standing with us were Rachel Stephens, Etheline Holder, and Barbara Bamberger, women who had become 'mothers in God' to us, and who would now take solemn promises to be the 'godmothers' of our son.

I saw it as a sign of wonder and of hope that a small baby who up until the time of birth knew only the life of the womb, is at baptism surrounded by life-giving women and life-affirming promises. I had planned that Themba should be baptised in the same gown that eight of my siblings had been baptized in back in South Africa, but the gown was lost in the post somewhere between Cape Town and London. The blue jump suit bought locally at short notice did not have the same sentimental value, but even so I knew that the promise held true – that all shall be well. My heart sang as the candle was lit and handed over with the words, "Themba, receive this light, for you belong to Christ the LIGHT of the world." My silent prayer was then, and continues to be, that my son whom I love so dearly may grow and live in the faith of Christ.

Children can be a blessing in so many ways, and one of the blessings that followed Themba's birth was that he was the means of further strengthening my relationship with Mark's Mum, Gladys. A loving bond had slowly developed between us, and over the years, whenever she phoned Mark, she would also spend some time talking with me. Mummy Sweet came from South Africa to visit us not long after Themba was born; he captured her heart, and she was a doting, helpful grandma. She fed him his first spoonful of solid food and coaxed and coo-ed until he voluntarily opened his mouth in that messy way that all babies have at the age of three months. She visited us on two more occasions while Themba was still young and was always a willing baby sitter when Mark and I had to travel to London for ANC meetings.

As time passed, Mark's absences were increasing all the time, and it seemed sometimes that I was having to be both mother and father to our son. There was some relief for a time when my mother came to stay with us, but that was only temporary. I had such fun with my mother, having known life only in South Africa, and only under apartheid, she found it difficult not to stare when she sees a mixed-race couple holding hands, or kissing each other on the underground station. Not only did she openly stare, she also tugged at my hand and quite audibly remarked: "Jenni, look, just look at them, hi can they do that here?" ... I would rebuke her in Afrikaans and tell her not to be so obvious! My friends loved my Mum and she got lots of invitations while she was over here. The fun part – or rather not so much fun as expensive – was when it was time for Mummy to go back to Cape Town. She had double the luggage she came with; wherever she visited she was given gifts and of course, the markets and charity shops were like magnets for my Mum. Her excuse was that she will not be accused of favouritism and so she must get something small for every member of the family. This inevitably meant extra suitcases which had to be paid for by us at the airport. Those are my good memories of my parents and parents-in-law honouring our home in England with their loving presence. Life was good, we had a place to stay, there was always enough food in the house and little Themba was growing up into a fine sociable toddler.

* * *

In many ways it was an exhilarating time, and looking back I am amazed at the range of people I met and the enriching experiences that I took part in. I was asked by the ANC Offices to represent our Movement at National events; at meetings of the British Trade Union Movement, including, once, at their Annual Conference in Blackpool; meeting with NGO's; at meetings of large and small groups in colleges and universities; at gatherings of churches of different denominations and on different scales, from single congregations to large conferences and celebrations. I shared platforms with representatives from other organisations such as SWAPO, OXFAM, Amnesty International, SHELTER, and the Anti-Apartheid Movement (UK).

I felt deeply honoured and immensely privileged to have been able to carry that responsibility on behalf of our people. Especially on behalf of the 'unsung heroes' of our struggle; the countless women and men whose names, sadly, will never be recognised on the world stage or even within South Africa itself. They are not known, but their legacy is known by people like myself. It was on their behalf that I found myself travelling around Britain as well as to Corrymeela in Northern Ireland.

It was in Corrymeela in 1987 that I had the great privilege of

With Dr Beyers Naudé, the well know Afrikaans cleric who played a crucial role in the South African churches' struggle against Apartheid

sharing a platform with Beyers Naudé (*Oom Bey*, as he was affectionately known) as we took part in a Seminar about War and Peace, sharing our understanding of a Just War from a South African perspective. I cannot now remember much of what Oom Bey said, but I do remember how much of what he said at the time resonated with me. I have always seen it as a miracle of Grace that a man like Beyers Naudé, of Afrikaner stock, should have understood so completely that as a follower of Jesus he had to use every effort to break down the evil structures of Apartheid. He is for me one of the icons of the struggle, and I look to him with admiration and deep respect. I too, was asked many times, how do I reconcile being a follower of Jesus and being a member of an organisation that resort to the use of firearms, weapons that kill? My response was that I became a member of the ANC because there never was asked of me to take up a gun, nor was that a prerequisite for joining the ANC. I tell people that at the time, the ANC stood for the Kingdom Values of the Gospel I believe in; the value of respect for each human being, that we are all equal before God, that we all have a human right to a decent home, a fulfilling job, we all must have enough to eat, that our land belongs to all of us who live and worked on it. That in Jesus Christ there is no superiority in being white skin and inferiority in having a black skin. I tell people that we, as a people's movement, we worked on four fronts (pillars). Those are:

- Mobilise the masses (worked at the grassroot level)
- Our underground movement (spearheaded civil disobedience, local boycotts, etc.)
- International solidarity (sanctions against South Africa, by our supporters overseas)
- Eventually the armed struggle.

Only after many years of unarmed confrontations against

the might of the apartheid state with it's military, SA Defence Force, armed white civilians, etc., the ANC made a decision to form Umkonto we Sizwe (the armed wing of the Movement). This was to defend and to protect ourselves. In the same way that the Afrikaners formed a laager and protected their loved ones during the Boer/Zulu wars. I believe that our people had the right to defend themselves, taking up arms as a last resort, taken not out of selfish desires, but for the benefit of the oppressed majority. I cannot, and will not, as a disciple of Jesus take up arms, but I do not judge those who have chosen to do so when finding themselves in a desperate situation.

I became one of the key speakers for the ANC and I publicly confessed my allegiance to Jesus Christ and his teachings. It was important for me to say it repeatedly and for people to hear that it was my faith that motivated me to speak into a political situation that had hundreds of souls languishing in prison, and hundreds more scattered across the world, living in exile away from their families; and the many who already have made the ultimate sacrifice. So, I did what I did in faith, never wavering, always with the conviction and belief that discipleship has a cost. I also knew that I never walked alone, for God was with me, and He would take care of me as He had during my brief spell in jail, as He had when I found myself in this country, far away from home and family.

To live, and to speak out in the knowledge that our aim was to have a free country and a better life for all of us, gave me a clear focus. I was not, and still am not, comfortable with being in the spotlight, but every invitation I received, was saturated in prayer; asking for grace, asking for confidence to be given to me, asking that I do not make a fool of myself and bring shame to God and the people I claimed to represent.

It was not an easy life. For every speaking engagement there was a lot of prior preparation, trying to keep up as events unfolded at home, checking the facts with comrades who would not always be in London conveniently when I needed to contact them, and I therefore had to pay out of my own pocket the cost of international phone calls. Then too, whenever there was a call for financial help for a fallen comrade's family we contributed as much as we could. On top of that, we always stood in solidarity with the people at home, as when in 1985, the call went out for a "black Christmas" as a black nation we were in mourning, and the people were asked not to decorate their homes, not to have festive feasts. We too, had a black Christmas in snow clad London – no Christmas tree, no special treats, no presents. Our little family had a meal of *samp* and beans on Christmas Day.

Mark, Themba and I had only one holiday together in all that time, and that sole occurrence was in the year that Themba turned two, when dear friends in Switzerland bought us tickets to come and visit them. It was our first and last family holiday!

We built up a wide social network, but our main focus was the work of the ANC and the exiled South African community. We worked hard here in Britain. Mark dedicated his life fully to the work of SACTU and the ANC. In between his travels to Eastern Europe, the Soviet Union, and the Balkan countries, he was writing from morning until night, producing teaching materials for the underground movement at home.

* * *

In the spring of 1987, it was confirmed that I had been accepted as a candidate for the ministry of the Methodist Church, and that in September of that year I would begin my three-year course of initial training at Wesley College, Bristol. Through all the rigorous tests and interviews that preceded that letter confirming my acceptance, Mark had been proudly supportive of everything I undertook. He even listens patiently as I read out my sermons before I preached, and sometimes would make insightful suggestions. He was my number one fan and I remember him for that.

When the time came for us to leave Notting Hill and move to Bristol, Mark took a year's furlough, so that he could look after our two-year-old toddler, Themba, and I could be freer to concentrate on fulltime studies. Mark recognised that for the preceding two years I had been the central person in Themba's life, and now he was ready to play a fuller role. He did an amazing job and a strong bond developed between father and son in the next few years.

Angry Love

Chapter 7
Training and Transformation

Wesley College in Bristol was situated in one of the most desirable parts of the city. It had its own campus, with rooms for lectures and seminars; a dining hall; accommodation for students (mainly in a residential block of flats); houses for the staff; and a Chapel for the whole community.

The courses offered to students preparing to become ministers in the Methodist Church were much more 'academic' than the ones I had taken at the Urban Theology Unit in Sheffield, or the Selly Oak Colleges in Birmingham. In some modules we were taught alongside students from the University and from the nearby training colleges of other churches and denominations; and sometimes students from Wesley College were enrolled for courses that ran at the University. I was really pleased when it was agreed that I could take part in the studies in Liberation Theology that the University offered.

My reaction to my studies reflected the mixed-up stage that I was at emotionally, spiritually and intellectually. I was challenged by the academic rigour that was required, but also, if I'm honest, a bit intimidated; I felt angry when I heard things being said, by tutors or by fellow students, that seemed to be far removed from the 'reality' of ordinary living, let alone the struggle to be freed from oppression; above all, I longed for the kind of learning that could be transformative, for me and for the communities that I would serve. I became good friends with some of those who studied with me, and years later, they told me that they had all been slightly afraid of the fiery Jenni Sweet, who at times could be anything but sweet!

We were expected to continue to preach and to lead worship while we were going through our three years of initial formation for ministry. It was enriching to be sent to a variety of churches and chapels in and around Bristol, and even 'over the border' into Wales. Life on campus was varied and full of its own difficulties and dramas: inevitable really, when people from a variety of backgrounds have to live so close to one another for extended periods. We sometimes got to know more about one another than we wanted to.

Another Party

Themba was two years old when we moved to Bristol, and he quickly got to know the other children around the campus and they all played together happily, with the older ones looking after the younger ones. It was a safe place to be, and I never felt any anxiety about how he was getting on. Then one day when I returned from lectures, as I approached the building where we lived, I saw Themba peering around the corner of the building, looking wistfully at a group of children who were wearing party hats and playing games, celebrating the birthday of one of them. I asked Themba why he wasn't with the other children, and very quietly he replied. "They didn't call me."

I felt so hurt for my son as I saw the questions in his eyes, and with a lump in my throat I hugged him, grabbed his hand and told him that we will have a special party. Just me and him! We took a bus into town and went to the Wimpy Bar and told Themba that he could choose whatever he wanted. He chose fish and chips; and I made sure that he also had a huge ice cream cone with a flake. Was it an oversight that my son was not invited to the party when all the other children were, or was it a conscious decision? Am I back in apartheid South Africa? I did not ask; I'll never know. I was surprised and disappointed that this had happened in a place where people were preparing for ministry in a diverse society. I could not imagine something like that happening in any of the places I had lived until then not in Sheffield, Notting Hill, or Selly Oak. I was learning all the time, and not only in the lecture rooms, that as a woman of colour I am bound to experience racism and prejudice, but I have to teach myself (and my beloved son) how to respond with grace and understanding.

The agreement that Mark should take a furlough from SACTU for a year and look after Themba while I studied, worked well. But Mark could not just drop everything that he had been doing in the years before my ministerial training began. We therefore tried to plan things so that he could be away at least for limited periods. It was during one of the times when Mark was away to a camp somewhere in Lusaka where our comrades were offered refuge – that the most traumatic of all that I have experienced in the struggle took place. I was made acutely aware, not only of just how vulnerable we were as a family, but also how far reaching the tentacles of the apartheid regime stretched.

Kidnapped

There was one day towards the end of my second year of training, June 1989, which was to become a day that I would never forget. It was a Friday, and the College was closing for the long summer holidays. A few of the students had left already for their summer holidays, and most of the rest were leaving on Saturday, the day after. It was one of those warm, languid mornings (balmy, as the English say). Everything was bright with sunlight, the trees outside our window were swaying in a gentle breeze; all was calm and there seemed to be a good and happy feeling even in the air.

For about three weeks there had been staying with us in our flat, a comrade who Mark and I had always known simply as Bassie. Mark had had to leave for ANC business in Lusaka during Bassie's stay, and on Saturday Bassie was due to leave for Moscow. On the Friday morning, I took Bassie with me to the nursery school, introduced him to the teacher, and explained that he would pick up Themba from school that afternoon, as I had a tutorial that meant I couldn't get to the nursery by its closing time of 3.15 p.m. With these arrangements in place, I went happily to my final tutorial of the term, confident that Themba would be back at home before my tutorial ended. But my son never returned home that day. He was kidnapped. Taken by the very person I trusted!

At first, I wasn't too concerned when I returned home and found the flat empty. I assumed that Bassie had taken Themba for a walk, or perhaps to the shops for an ice cream. But by six o' clock that evening I was becoming anxious that there was still no sign of Bassie or Themba. By a quarter to nine that night, having knocked on every door on the campus and spoken to Themba's little friends and parents, I found myself at the local police station making a statement about what had happened so far that day.

The policeman at the desk explained that I would have to wait twenty-four hours before a missing person's file could be opened. I was horrified and I refused to leave the police station and to come back later, as he suggested. I sat there and insisted that he phoned around to other police stations and alert them to be on the look-out for a man of about forty years, and a small boy of four and a half. I felt sick in the pit of my stomach; I felt as if I was in a nightmare, and my normal world was shattered to smithereens.

Up to this day I cannot give a coherent picture of what exactly happened that night. Only that I was conscious of grabbing hold of the policeman's hand and begging him, pleading with him, to find my child. By that time, I was howling like an animal, screaming like a demented person "Please, GOD ... my child! Please, GOD, protect my child!"

Even in that time of deepest darkness, there was a glimmer of light which came through the policeman: he made contact with my parents in South Africa, and passed the phone over to me. I was unable to speak coherently, gasping and sobbing, and could only manage to utter a word or two before dissolving into a blubbering mess. The angel policeman took back the phone and explained the situation. He asked my father to contact Mark's parents, and assured my Dad that they (the police) would do their utmost to find Themba. "Tell them to pray; tell them to pray", I whimpered at the policeman's shoulder.

The voice of prayer is never silent. Within minutes, as the news was filtered through to our families, friends and church fellowship, the earth reverberated with Grace as anguished beseeching prayers were sent out to reach God's ears and heart. Christians and Moslems at home, with the church communities in the UK, formed a prayer chain that continued throughout the night and into the next day. During those twenty-six hours of waiting, it was as if I was in a void – while others prayed. I did not know how to pray. The words that came so easily when I was at the bedside of a sick person, or dealing with a difficult pastoral situation, just did not come this time. I was bereft of words. Words were in the way. Words made no sense. I began to tumble into a deep pit of agony and fear for my son's safety.

Dim, flickering images and faint words occasionally filtered through the darkness. I remember the kindness on the face of the policeman after he saw how panic-stricken and heart-broken I was, and realised that the situation could be really grave. I remember, too, the expression on the face of the Tutor from the College who had accompanied me to the police station: he was clearly feeling out of his depth, and seemed to be pleading: "What am I supposed to do?" And I remember his words: "Trust God, Jenni, just trust in Him. That's all you can do now." And that's exactly what I did. I just gave it over to God.

After twenty-six hours in which words held no meaning, twenty-six hours in which I became oblivious to everything and everyone around me – except for the non-stop refrain in my head, "Please, God, please God, protect my son; please God hold him, please...please". After what seemed like an eternity, I was able to hold my son in my arms once more.

Through the combined work of the British Police, detectives and the Security Service, bolstered I believe by the prayers of believers, Bassie had been picked up at Victoria Station, waiting, with Themba beside him, to get on a bus heading for the West of England. Themba, it has to said, did not appear unduly concerned about what had happened; he was with someone he knew and trusted, someone who had been staying in his home, so when 'Uncle Bassie' told him that they were going on a trip, Themba had simply accepted it.

* * *

Over the next few weeks, the story behind the kidnapping gradually emerged. We discovered that Bassie was suspected of being an informer who infiltrated ANC gatherings and befriended comrades living in the UK, so as to supply information to the Special Branch in South Africa. I shudder at our naivety – to think that we welcomed him into our home; we left him in charge of our most precious gift, our son. But we saw him as a comrade, fighting for the same goals we were fighting for! Someone to be trusted. I saw him as someone who came 'from home', a friend who ate the food I cooked for three weeks, whose clothes I washed with ours in the washing machine. Someone who spoke Afrikaans to me and laughed at anecdotes I shared about my family. This was a friend who, for three weeks, slept in Themba's bedroom, and who argued, debated and bantered with Mark way into the night. I felt so betrayed!

Our son was an innocent child being used in political machinations that he knew nothing about. For a child to be used in this way is unforgivable, and no mother, no parent, should be put through such agonising hell – ever!

It was a long time before I could begin to see how much grace was revealed and experienced even through this traumatic event. From deep inside me I know that God was at work in all that happened that day. I know that God heard our cries and I know that his Grace was seen in the actions of strangers, friends and the police. I know that I'm no-one special, but I know that I have experienced God's Grace, special and undeserved, that comes freely to people who do not deserve it. I am one of those people. I know more than anything else that whenever I have found the courage to do what is right in spite of the cost – that has been because of grace; and whenever people have said how commendable it is that I have been able to forgive Basie, that too, has been a gift of grace.

Grace makes it possible to forgive the person who kidnaps your only son. Grace allows for sensitivity towards the person who discriminates against you because of your skin colour, or your religion. Grace changed my life completely and, looking back, I can trace how in myriad ways my life was enriched by a Higher Source that lies beyond me. I cannot speak academically or objectively about grace but I can speak from my heart, from my own experience, about the times when I have been the recipient of God's grace, and I began to do that more and more after the traumatic incident of Themba's kidnapping.

Within the College, the agony of that terrible ordeal created what I call a 'Ribbon of Grace' around our family; my fellow student ministers and their families, the College Tutors and the whole college community showed exceptional support and care for Themba, Mark and myself throughout the rest of my time at Wesley College. Prayers were offered for us regularly in the College prayers that were held on Wednesday evenings, and to our names would be added those of other families whose children went missing, some of whom were never heard of again. People went out of their way to make us know that they were there for us, sometimes by pushing through our letterbox some comforting and uplifting words of Scripture, or by leaving carefully wrapped on our doorstep a cake or a roasted chicken – often without any name to show who it was from. There was an increased watchfulness on the part of the community, and there was a readiness to ensure that people coming onto the campus had good reasons for being there. It was like having our own plain clothes police force!

The College decided that they would show their support for the struggle for liberation in a very practical way by allowing the ANC Unit to which Mark and I belonged to have a room free of charge at the College for their monthly meetings. This was a great help as it meant that comrades in and around Bristol no longer had to travel to London for Unit meetings. To add to this generosity, some of the student households would provide meals for the comrades attending these meetings.

It was another lesson learned outside of the classroom, that pain and suffering can carry seeds of redemption within them, and grace can grow even where the soil seems least fertile.

Celebration

On February 1990, Nelson Mandela was released from prison after spending twenty-seven years behind bars. The announcement was heard around the world; every channel, every station, carried the news – and the celebrations began!

It was about seven o'clock in the morning when I received a call from the Bristol Anti-Apartheid Group, telling me that I must come immediately to the town centre; they were sending a cab to pick me up. I dressed hurriedly and jumped into the cab that arrived almost as the call ended. As we approached College Green, a huge park in the centre of Bristol, we could see a large crowd gathering, swelling each moment as more and more people came from all directions, winding their way to College Green. Some were waving ANC flags, and others, mainly students, were doing their version of the South African 'toyi-toyi' dance. The atmosphere was electric; the feeling ecstatic! It was like being caught up in an early morning picnic party.

Before I could even collect my thoughts there was an announcement over the public address system that Jenni Sweet from the ANC would now speak, and a loud cheer went up. I cannot remember what I said that day, I had no time to prepare; I didn't expect to be asked to speak at such an historic moment. I know there must have been South Africans among the thousands of people there that morning, because at the end of my speech, someone started singing *Nkosi Sikelel' iAfrika*. The crowd took up the tune, even though most didn't know the words, and the sound of our celebration was sent heavenwards, and I'm sure that even the angels felt they had to join in the song, 'God, bless Afrika'.

Back down on earth, the day passed in a blur: an interview on Local Radio (Bristol); joy and celebrations all around the College throughout the day; calls to South Africa; a day of rejoicing.

In the weeks that followed there were more speaking and preaching engagements, at St Martin-in-the-Field, London; to small groups that I had come to know well, and to large crowds full of people that I didn't know, all wanting to hear about the new dawn in South Africa.

A few months later, an event was held in Chantilly, France, that was especially memorable. There was still a lot of euphoria at the release of Nelson Mandela, and I was attending as a participant and as one of the speakers representing the ANC. When the time came for me to speak in one of the workshops, as I approached the platform, someone shouted "Mandela's Woman!" This shout was taken up and then more and more voices started chanting, "Mandela's woman! Mandela's Woman!" It was an unbelievable experience, made more

On the occasion of the State visit of Pres. Nelson Mandela in the company of Her Majesty the Queen. Outside Royal Albert Hall with Vesta Smith (member of FEDSAW (Federation of South African Women) & members of Christian Fellowship Trust (UK).

powerful by it being so spontaneous. "Mandela's Woman" stood in front of that excited crowd, and rather than raising her fist and shouting back 'Amandla!' (Power!) as she might have done on other occasions, she was sobbing uncontrollably, and completely unable to begin her speech! I have never felt so humbled, so inadequate and so powerful as at that moment in

Angry Love

a hall full of strangers, in a faraway land.

My time of training had been a time of transformation in so many different ways.

Angry Love

Chapter 8
Ministry, for all

At the end of their time of initial training, Student Ministers in the Methodist Church are sent to their first appointment as Probationer Ministers, where they will have 'pastoral responsibility' for one Church, or often more than one, and are expected to continue to learn and be formed as ministers under the watchful eye of a Superintendent Minister. The church goes to great lengths to make sure that the churches that Probationer Ministers are sent to, are ones that are suited to their gifts and abilities, and that will also allow them to grow.

When my course of training ended in the summer of 1990, the appointment chosen for me was to be responsible for two churches in Tottenham, North London, and one of those churches was adjacent to the Broadwater Farm estate. The name Broadwater Farm had become notorious as the place where two years previously there had been an eruption of racial riots, and a policeman was shot and killed by someone in the crowd. The 'powers that be' in the church had decided that I was the 'right' person to be the minister of the Methodist Church in that situation, so in August 1990, we moved as a family from the quiet leafy avenues in Bristol that had been our home for three years, to the intensity and bustle of a London inner city Borough.

Feelings were still raw among the worshippers and the atmosphere in the church and in the community was tense. Many of those who attended the Methodist Church knew of someone who had been involved in the riots, and some had family members who were in jail as a result of things that happened during the riots. The leaders in the church sensitively spelt out the situation between police and the local community and assured me of their support for me as the Minister who will be pastorally responsible for families on either side of the divide. I was made aware of the huge task upon my shoulders, to bring about peace and reconciliation among a community divided against itself. I felt a sinking feeling of '*déjà vu*' and must admit there was a certain lack of enthusiasm for this, my very first Circuit appointment.

Beginnings

When a minister begins serving in a new place, it is a custom to have a 'Welcome Service' for them and their family. This will be attended not just by members of the church(es) that the minister will be responsible for, but by members from other churches in the Circuit and by religious leaders from other churches and Faiths. Often the Mayor of the Borough, local dignitaries and community and civic leaders will be invited; and often, also, there will be a guest speaker invited for the occasion.

I was ecstatic to learn that the preacher for my welcome service would be Father Trevor Huddleston! He is a Priest who has a remarkable reputation worldwide, but to me he was a colleague who had become a friend and confidant to Mark as well as me. People all over the world will remember him as the one whom Bishop Desmond Tutu referred to as "the white priest who doffed his hat" in greeting to the Archbishop's mother. For me, having Trevor Huddleston as the Preacher at my welcome service was yet another gift of Grace; I couldn't have asked for a more affirming start to my time as a Circuit Minister.

We soon settled as a family into the spacious Manse that was provided for us, just a few doors away from the church, and Mark resumed his work with the South African Congress of Trade Unions in London. We felt that it was important for Themba to feel secure in his school environment, and for us to know that he was safe and protected. (We were still haunted by the memory of his abduction, and were not sure whether there might be longer term implications for Themba also). We decided to send him to a small preparatory school where, we hoped, with smaller classes (fifteen children per class) he would be more likely to receive individual attention from a caring teacher when necessary. The one drawback was that the school was ten miles away and I didn't drive. In spite of that it turned out to be a good choice for Themba and he enjoyed making new friends and taking part in all that the school had to offer.

* * *

In the meantime, I was warmly welcomed into the church which had over a hundred members – which was large by comparison with many other churches at that time; it also had a thriving Sunday School and a Boys Brigade company. Life took on a busy rhythm of holding together school runs and domestic responsibilities, alongside a church ministry that required caring for members and adherents while also working out the Gospel command to make peace where there is strife.

I quickly became involved in bringing different factions together, using music (we held musical concerts in the church hall, got local young people to come and play drums, or whatever instrument, in church services), to promote cross cultural understanding and harmony in the community. It was a difficult time for many families who were caught up in the riots and suffered personal tragedy either through violent death during the fighting on the Estate or had spent considerable time in hospital after an operation to put their bodies back together again.

The local clergy, myself included, held a round table with members of the Community and, with the help of an agency called Y Care, were able to provide support for young people living on the Estate, enabling them to grow trees, plant flower beds and create lawns. This gardening project and the music workshops, became a focus for bringing the community together and a step towards healing the rifts. When the green grass started to grow and the colourful flowers burst open, it immediately gave a more welcoming image, contrasting with the dull white of the concrete slabs that was home to a wide range of nationalities and cultures.

I have found that to build trust in a community filled with mistrust and fear, takes up a lot of energy and giving of self. I have learnt that the problems of human nature, the good and bad in all of us, will continue to exist, even within the most sophisticated of self-help programmes. I enjoyed my ministry in Tottenham and working from a church base with the wider community was both satisfying and challenging. I was anxious to do my best; I wanted to meet the many demands of ministry as best I could, being the kind of person who finds it difficult to say no to anyone 'who needs me'.

Reaching Out

One of the aspects of being a Methodist Minister that was inescapable in my training, is that ministry is for ALL. It was there in the lectures, in the seminars and tutorials, in the hymns we sang in worship. This was a view of ministry that I found totally convincing and appealing, and I embraced it completely. One of the best-known quotes from John Wesley is his claim: "The world is my parish." My 'parish' began to reach, not just beyond the ring of the church community, but beyond the borders of Tottenham!

The continued interest in South Africa, heightened by the release of Mandela in the very year I came to Tottenham, meant that there was an endless stream of invitations for me, as someone who was a South African, woman of colour, Minister, to speak at all kinds of events. Wherever I went, the audiences were eager to know more about my beloved country, and news reports of the atrocities inherent of that abhorrent system, did not endear South Africa to British people.

I addressed the PCR Special (for women only) Conference on Racism at one of their meetings in Chantilly. I spoke at the Green Belt Festival, a national gathering of people of all faiths, held annually in the country of Kent and had following me on the programme, Cliff Richard, who began his session by commending warmly what he had heard me say while he was waiting to come on stage! I was interviewed on BBC Radio 4, during "Woman's Hour" which, I'm told, had a following of several million at that time. There was a tree planting ceremony

With fellow speakers at a conference on NGO's and the challenge of poverty and homelessness.

in St James's Park, where I was alongside Nelson Mandela and members of the Executive of the ANC, including the 'Chief Whip' of the ANC in London, comrade Mendi Msameng, and this was followed by breakfast, hosted by Prince Charles, with Archbishop Ramsay also present.

Angry Love

We tried as far as it was possible to live out the pledge we made as part of our marriage vows, that our home would be home for all those who have no place to call home. During our time in Tottenham we welcomed so many people into our home that I could not possibly now remember all their names. However, I do remember that one evening Mark phoned and asked me to cook 'a nice meal' as he was bringing three Trade Union comrades home for dinner. That evening my common lentil stew was elevated to 'a struggle meal', shared with Jay Naidoo, Bob Marley (the nick-name of one comrade) and Cyril Ramaphosa (who, I think, became quite well known later!). Our home became for many of the comrades who passed through London to other European destinations, a place for the 'gathering of the clan'. I felt like a mother hen and it was a joy and a privilege to open our doors wide and offer hospitality to, among others; Hantie Kotze, Russell Botman, Vesta Smith, Chris and Annemarie Spies, in typical South African style, with food, music, dancing, and loud laughter.

And in the midst of all this, I continued, without fail, to fulfil my responsibilities as a Circuit minister, and to seek to serve each member to the best of my ability. I tried to make sure that, in the words of the 'charge' given to ministers, 'none suffer neglect'. It was a demanding time, and looking back, I realised that it was then that I began to take Mark for granted. I did not fully appreciate what he was doing to help me fulfil my responsibilities as the Minister of a growing Church. The church took over my life and more and more Mark was left to fend for himself and Themba while I had to rush to yet another pastoral emergency. Added to my ministerial demands was the string of invitations from different denominations who wanted to have special thanksgiving services for the release of Nelson Mandela, and would I please come and preach. I suppose it all went to my head a little bit, because I was suddenly thrown into the limelight as the 'feisty South African woman with her fist in the air" and so all this speaking and preaching engagements took precedence over my role as a mother and as a wife. I was probably spending more time in other people's homes than I spent in my own.

Pain and Loss

It was during our second year in Tottenham that I noticed a change in Mark. He became withdrawn, not saying very much. I put it down to the changing situation back home in South

Africa. With the release of Nelson Mandela, there was much talk among the ANC cadres in the UK about returning home, some of the black comrades who have gained degrees from British universities, were already applying for jobs at home. Mark had always held the view that as a white South African, he had had a better education than the black comrades he was working with, so when invitations to study in different European countries were extended to members of the Liberation Movement, he felt those opportunities should be given to the black comrades. This meant that while others gained one degree after another, Mark doggedly and consistently gave his time and skills and time to the work of the Movement, and in particular the trade union (SACTU).

We shared the household chores; we both enjoyed cooking our vegetarian meals and spent relaxing times around the table, each sharing stories of our day, and always the conversation inevitably came to focus on South Africa and what the future might hold for us now that Nelson Mandela was free. But this magical, happy family pattern slowly started to change. As the church calendar started to fill up, I was out of the house for as much as three evenings a week. Mark's work would also take him away for two to three days at a time, running workshops or doing other things related to his work.

One night, Mark arrived home from a meeting well past midnight. There was no anxiety in my mind because I knew from past experience that one can get carried away in political meetings, especially when that meeting consists of South Africans talking about South Africa. The following week the same thing happened. After a month of him arriving home past midnight at least once per week, I asked him what was happening. He said that after the meetings he gave comrades lifts home, and that by the time he'd dropped the two at their homes, and made his way back across London, it would naturally be after midnight.

* * *

It was now the year 1992. The year I spent in hell. Most of that year was lived in a mist of pain fog. During this time a friend gave me what is called "A Gratitude Journal". She said: "Jenni you must stop crying. You have much to be thankful for. Here, write in this diary something you are thankful for every day." This diary became my daily confessional and made up for the absence of my mother, and sisters to whom I would've confided in, had they been here. But they were far away and what was happening to me was so raw and immediate. Writing things down relieved some of the heaviness in my chest. I know now that hell is not that burning furnace from which anguish cries can be heard, but the burning excruciating pain within the human breast, and the daily silent cries of indescribable pain. Only the first three entries speak of thankfulness and gratitude. The rest reflects the misery I lived in. I wrote on:

Wednesday February 26: Thank you Lord for my warm bed. I like my bed; I can sink into its softness and warmth and I feel snug and warm. Thank you for toast and marmalade. Mark left the house at eight tonight. He returned 4am the next morning.

Saturday March 14: Thank you for candles. Warm glow and friendly. Nice smell. Thank you for my books and my eyes. Thank you for little Themba, my boy. My darling sweet boy. Thank you for giving him to me to take care of, Lord.

Friday March 20: I am grateful for this lovely home you gave us Lord. Thank you for hymns that I can sing to, thank you for my longarm music I can dance to. Thank you for food in the house. Thank you for my sisters and brothers.

Sunday March 29: Mothering Sunday: Will we spend today as a family? I made apple crumble, Mark's favourite but he's gone, like so many times before. Just left, said he's going to Orpington for a meeting. What can I thank you for today, Lord? I don't know... I wish I can stop this crying... This pain inside is swelling bigger and bigger every day. I ache. My stomach ache. My whole body is aching. Mark ... Mark! I cry inside. Every day as I walk, talk to people another voice in my head cries Mark. And every night I cry his name before you and into my pillow. Please give me your peace, Lord.

Friday April 10: It is now 2am in the morning. Where is he Lord? Where does my husband go to night after night, and I can't ask him because I'm too full of tears. I chased Themba to bed so that I can sit here on the stairs to cry. Alone. I am so alone. All the time. Where are you, Mark? What have I done to you? What is going on...??

Saturday April 18: I married Margaret and Colin today. Mark was there, in church. He was invited to the wedding and reception. We sat next to each other and yet our spirits were far away from each other. He brought me home around 11:30pm, opened the door and kissed me on the cheek and said "I'm just going for a drive, see you later" and promptly left. I lie awake until 5am when I heard his key in the door.

Friday May 2nd: May Day. International Workers Day, we were both invited as members of the ANC to this celebration where Mark was one of the Speakers. It was held in Conway Hall, Red

Lion Square in London. Music, dance, food from around the world. ANC choir sang beautifully and brought tears to many eyes including mine. Mark arranged for one of the comrades to bring me and Themba home. He returned Sunday morning around 8am.

June to August: My diary entries speak of Mark coming and going, of me crying incessantly and us not communicating at all. When I do try to speak to Mark, I start to cry and Mark then say he cannot talk to me while I'm like this. Themba was the only person we both speak with, and care for and pour our love over.

Tuesday September 29: I took Themba to school. He said where is Dad? Why is he not taking me to school today? I told him Dad is busy, but will pick him up from school. My sweet boy was happy. I watched as he skipped off through the school gates with his friends. He is so like Mark, the way he moves his head, the way he looks at me when I speak to him, with such a clear, unwavering stare giving me his full attention. You are precious to me my boy. Dad and I made you when we thought we would always be happy together. You help me to remember the good times, Themba. And you also help me to forget what is happening to us now... Be good my boy, grow up to be beautiful and strong. Be kind to people. Just like your Dad.

Saturday October 10: Mark went to one of the comrade's party tonight without me. I asked to go with; I know this comrade. He said I can't because I'm a minister in the church. He never said that before, we always went to parties together, why can't a minister attend a party? I always have. I do. Why does he not want me with him, I asked. He just looked at me and said "you know why" – and walked out of the door. I cried myself to sleep...

Tuesday November 3rd: I got my drivers-license today. When my driving instructor said you have passed your test, I burst into tears. He didn't really know what to do, just stared at me uncomfortably and said 'there, there, it's not the end of the world". I think he was relieved when I got out of the car. I cried because Mark has been away for two days now and there was no phone call, and I haven't slept well the past three days.

My diary entries continued in similar vein until February 1993.

I was in such a state, I didn't know how or what to do. The constant pain in my chest intensified, and my anxiousness increased, as one night per week became three, and Mark's time of return got later and later, sometimes stretching to four and five o'clock in the morning. This continued for the rest of that year. A year in which I found myself walking around with clenched fists, and my eyes screwed up into tiny slits. During this time, I seldom slept a full night, and for a time I popped Valiums to help me sleep. But the doctor refused to give me any more when I asked for a repeat prescription. I asked questions over and over; I guess I started nagging: "Where have you been? Why are you so late? Who have you been with? Who did you give a lift to?" Mark just maintained a stony silence. He refused to talk. All my numerous attempts to get some sort of dialogue going, some verbal response, came to nothing.

* * *

Then, one day when he sat in front of his computer (this happened frequently – when he was in the house he would go immediately to his computer and open it up), as I stood at the door, speaking to him and he didn't look up. He didn't even acknowledge that I was there in the room with him. He stared fixedly at the computer screen as I was talking to him. Something snapped inside me. I walked up to him as he sat there and slapped him hard on the side of his face! I shall never forget the look on his face. White faced. Hard eyes like flintstones. There was hatred written on his face. "Don't you ever lift your hands to me again. Ever! I hate you!" he cried, grabbed his jacket off the chair and stormed out of the house. He didn't return until two days later. We settled into a pattern of sullen silence, the atmosphere heavy with unspoken words and questions. The only words Mark did say was to say thank you after a meal. No matter what we ate or when, he would always say thank you to me. We both spoke only to Themba.

My life took on a nightmarish quality. I continued to preach every Sunday, conduct weddings, organise funerals and led the Church Council, Leaders Meeting, Ladies Fellowship. I offered pastoral care and presided at Holy Communion – everything was done in a misty haze; everything took on a dreamlike state. How I managed, how I got through that year is known only to God. I prayed, oh how I prayed. I don't remember what words I used, I only remember sobbing before God and saying the same words over and over again: "Please God, bring my husband back. Bring him back. Restore our marriage" ... For the rest of that year, I hardly slept and existed in the nightmare of my husband sleeping somewhere else and arriving in our home as if there was nothing wrong. Mark started to wear new shirts, a new jacket. I took a pair of scissors, cut them in shreds and put them back in the drawer. I was like a mad woman living in a world of shadows. By this time, I was so unhinged, I went through his brief case, and another day I went through his pockets and found two (used) adult tickets for a train journey to Brighton.

* * *

Mark stopped coming to church with us, and our home became a place where he would sometimes stop off to eat, and to sleep in the study. He continued to take Themba to school. But he didn't look happy, there was an atmosphere of sadness hanging around him. He looked as if he was carrying the world on his shoulders. He became a shadow of his former self. I felt sorry for him; I needed to help him, but I couldn't help him. There was no way I could help while he was leading a double life that was cutting me up. I knew I was broken, screaming inside whilst keeping up appearances. I was functioning in a state of shock but with an all-pervasive sense of duty to my church and the determination that 'the show must go on.'

But I broke down in the supermarket when my hand automatically reached for Mark's favourite muesli. I vomited in the church toilet after I performed a wedding. I cried more than the grieving families when I did funeral services. There were times when I despised myself for falling apart. "Where is your faith?" I asked myself? I prayed feverishly that God should intervene and send Mark back to us. I read the Bible but nothing made sense. When it was day, I prayed for night to come; and when it was night, I would lie awake waiting for daylight. I realised that Mark was drifting away from me, but I still loved him. I also realised that he is in pain too; I carried hope in my heart that all shall be well, I just have to pray more. To stay calm and not cry so much. I didn't know how to stop loving Mark. I have loved him for so long and I cannot imagine my life without him. I cried so much all the time; I cried when I did the shopping, I cried in the still hours of the night. I cried when I was preparing a sermon or a talk. I had no defences; I didn't have the emotional tools to restrain myself. With hindsight I realised that I did all the wrong things I now tell other women NOT to do when they find themselves in similar situation.

* * *

Then Mark finally uttered the words that I dreaded to hear – that he was leaving. He said he was leaving because he needed space; that I was suffocating him, and he felt alienated in this marriage. He said that he'd given me all that he can, and I had dried him out. At that time, he never mentioned the word 'divorce'. All he wanted, he said, was time on his own.

Mark left for home on February 2nd 1993. The Movement needed him back home to help with the forthcoming elections ... Themba and I went to the airport to see him off. As he held Themba tightly to him, he was crying, and I heard him say that he will come back, that Themba must do well in school and to phone him when he needs help with his homework. He gave me a hug and said that as soon as he was settled with a job and had found a house, he would send for us. He said, "Jen, I must go home; there is nothing here for me. My place is with our comrades at home and I must help with next year's elections. Take care of yourself and Themba. I'll let you know how things are going". And he was gone.

* * *

Over the years that followed Mark's leaving, I had a lot of time to reflect. And I realised that I carry part of the blame for the breakdown of our marriage. I was the new Presbyter who was trying so hard to impress the congregation, and to show that I was a 'good' minister. It was my very first appointment as a probationer minister, and there were so many new things for me to learn: Everything I did in the ministry was my first: I conducted my first funeral; officiated at my first wedding; presided over my first Holy Communion, called and chaired my first Church Council, etc, etc. I cut my teeth and learned to walk as a minister in Miller Memorial Methodist Church.

I admit with shame that I did not support Mark in his political work with the trade union as much as I ought to have done. Because from where I was standing, it was the very same political work that took him away from us for weeks on end, going from one meeting to the next. I wanted a normal husband, with normal working hours, who would spend quality time with his wife and son. I wanted a life that was more 'normal', allowing, of course, for the few exceptional occasions when we would give some of our time to the Movement.

As for Mark, the Movement was the central thing; the cause to which he had devoted his life and for which he had sacrificed so much. The liberation of our people and country was his passion, his life.

* * *

My life was one of carefully balancing and juggling the roles of wife and parent; Minister of two churches; representing the ANC in response to the many invitations from schools, civic bodies, organisations and Churches across Britain. In that life I wanted, I needed and looked for, a husband who would be there to support me and who would help me to keep sane and secure when faced with the competing and growing demands. We both ended up not giving the other the support and understanding that we each craved for.

Themba and I had to find a way to live without Mark. It was hard for both of us. Themba retreated further into his shell. He was always a quiet child, not speaking much unless spoken to. I know he was grieving not only an absent Dad, but his hero. During one of the parent evenings, his teacher told me that Mark and the selfless work he does in the Struggle, was one of Themba's favourite topic of conversation for oral lessons in class. At nine years old, Themba was quite the little man. He felt that he had to protect me, look after me. He never shed tears in front of me, but they were there in his eyes, unshed and I knew he was suffering too. My heart just broke when I heard him sobbing in his bedroom late one night when he thought I was in my bedroom. I went in and held him tightly against me and my son said beautiful words to me: "Just pray to the good spirits Mum and they will bring Dad home again." Themba gave me the will to go on. When I thought it was the end of my world, he was there with childlike faith helping me to pick up the pieces.

In April 1994 Mark telephoned me to say that we (the ANC) had won by a clear majority; it was a landslide victory! Comrade Nelson Mandela became the people's president of South Africa. Mark said that he would come to London as soon as possible to pick up the books and stuff he had left behind with me. He added that there was something else he needed to say to me, but that it was best for that to be said face to face. But in my emotional state, I refused to consider his reasonable suggestion that we should wait for when we can sit down like adults and talk about the state of our marriage.

I insisted that I wanted to know now, not later whenever he can come to London. My heart was racing and palms were sweating as I gripped the phone. Mark then said that he didn't love me anymore; it felt as if something inside of me was tearing apart, as if muscle was ripped from my bone. He said that he hadn't loved me for a long time – and that he'd met someone else. He said that his new partner reminded him of me (!), that he loved her, and that I must try to get on with my life. He said that he was sorry; that I'd always be his friend and the care for me would still be there, just not as his wife. He asked that I should look after Themba and tell him that his Dad loves him. He would write to Themba as soon as he could. I didn't say a word, I tried to, but nothing came out except a strangled cry... He was still talking when I put the phone down and sank to my knees on the floor. And did what I have done for the past two years. I cried, screamed shrieked and afterwards, took deep breaths. And that's how I learnt to take deep breaths when I find the world closing in on me.

Well, he did write to Themba, and phoned him on his birthdays. He never wrote or spoke to me. I, on the other hand, wrote letter after letter to him saying how much I loved him, imploring him to come back, promising to be a better wife. Even though I've experienced Mark's coldness and indifference before he left, I still couldn't accept that Mark had left our marriage. Other men leave their wives, but not my gentle, kind and loving Mark! Mark will not leave his wife and child! I wrote letters reminding him of our love, of the times we cried together over the death of a loved one or comrade, of the happy times. Only one of my many letters was answered. Looking back on that dark period of brokenness, I can say without a doubt that it was grace, only grace, which brought me through. My diary became my daily confessor, I wrote ferociously and without restraint. There are too many anxious moments, and too many sleepless nights and too many difficult decisions I had to make as a single mother, telling them all would require a supplement to this chapter! Instead, I give expression to one of the many ways I coped, in this poem I wrote;

A POEM WITH NO NAME

There are certain things I know to be beautiful
and good and comforting,
And my inner being hunger after them,
Peace in my heart and things that bring
a smile to my lips;
The birds singing in the stillness of the early morning,
I give praise to God.
Bach's Brandenburg Concerto no 5 playing
when I bake apple crumble;
Themba singing way off key in the bathroom!

The memory of my husband's face when he looked
down at his son for the first time
– a tiny baby, with tiny hands, and one eye closed because
of the struggle to be born.
Tonight, like so many nights before I miss my husband.
I miss his arms around me, and the warmth
of his breath on my neck.
Dear Lord, I know you know everything,
but that doesn't take away my heartache,
Or the bleeding wound in my soul. Into the dark I scream
my muffled sobs;
Mark, where are you?... Mark...
Where are YOU Lord?? YOU have abandoned me.
I cannot feel you near me,
Nothing makes sense. I can't think straight.
I feel dejected, rejected:
People talk. They talk about Love, marriage,
divorce, so glibly.
Christian friends say to me there's a reason for all this,
there's something better round the corner.
I have to keep praying. Hope for the best. Believe that
God knows best...
All these religious platitudes, this sanctimonious jargon – I
hear them every day.

THEY ARE MEANINGLESS.
How can a love that was so beautiful,
something that felt so right?
bring such a pain like this?
A strange heavy pain like an elephant foot on my chest.
Difficult to breathe.
If it's your will God, you can take away this pain.
Smile, Themba is watching me.

Angry Love

There is sadness and pain in his eyes too,
Reflecting my own sadness. I look away.
I do not want to see the questions in my son's eyes.
I have my own questions.
There are so many demands on me:
Inside I scream go away, go away!
So many meetings: Property meeting,
Church Council Meetings, Women's Fellowship,
Bible Studies, Steward Meetings.
Meet with the scouts & the Girl Guides.
Babies to baptise, happy couples to marry.
The dead to be buried.
Meet with couple who lost their baby.
Meet with David he needs a character reference.
Meet with Fundraising Committee they
want to discuss the church bazaar.
Get up. Put on something pretty,
wear your clerical collar. Look normal,
No-one will know that you cracking up,
keep talking, keep praying, keep singing.
Just get through THIS day.

Though I felt that I was alone and had to fight the darkness on my own, that was not true. There were two 'angels', messengers of God, who ministered to me in those days of despair. The first was the Superintendent Minister of the Circuit, Rev Brian Goss; he was so patient, so gentle, so full of wisdom and understanding. He would insist that I should go with him to the park, and would listen while I talked; or he would buy me an ice cream, or a cup of tea, depending on the weather, would hold my hand in a kindly way and be not embarrassed by my tears, and he would pray with me.

The second angel was Vanessa, a member of another church, who saw me one night when I was really low. Again, she listened to me, prayed with me, and became a friend to me. Both Vanessa and Brian did their best to boost my self-esteem. From childhood I'd been made to feel that I wasn't as attractive as my sisters, and having my husband leave me for another woman just seemed to confirm that message. My two earthly angels told me that I was an attractive woman, that other women looked up to me and welcomed the ministry I offered. Vanessa and Brian bolstered my self-confidence, with encouraging words saying that I give people hope, and I help them walk closer to God. They both said I have something meaningful to offer other women.

At first it did not help. What help can I offer, I argued, when I'm in the state that I am? According to congregation, I am the one who has this direct line to God, so why can't I use it for myself, this lifeline that I throw to others? I tried to pray; I tried to see a way through, but nothing is there. I feel dead. Empty. What will happen if the church sees how frightened and unsure I am; what will happen when they realise that I paddle like a hamster on a wheel in this dark pit going round and round? Do they know that I find it difficult to pray; do they know that I am a fake?

Vanessa holds my hand and says: "Be strong, Jenni. You still have you. Have faith that all shall be well, and find joy in the knowledge that you are doing the best you can right now. Love yourself more; love your child, and love all the people around you who love you even though you don't think they do. You will survive, many women do. Take time with yourself. Let Mark go. Let him go; he wants to go, and if he loves you, he will come back."

He never did. And I survived.

I survived because, as before, God was there with me. In the mess, in the searing pain, in the long nights and in the full days. I took one step at a time. I lived one day at a time, and sang "God will take care of you." And, ever faithful, ever true, God did continue to take care of me; and God still does, and I'm sure now, will always do so.

* * *

It was around this time that, through the wisdom of my beloved son (that wisdom that Scripture tells us is given to young children and even babies not yet weaned!), I got another insight into what Grace means. One Sunday, Themba was with me in church, and must have been listening with extra attention at the end of the service, as I asked the congregation to bless each other by saying the Grace Blessing together.

As we were walking home, Themba turned to me and said: "Now I don't have to worry about you walking home alone, you have the angels going before you now, haven't you, Mum?" Puzzled, I looked at him, waiting for him to go on. "You've just ask for God's Grace, Mum; you're covered!" And then it dawned on me as I stared at my son's beautiful face so eager, so alight with love and life. I got! I got it, that when we say "And now may the grace of our Lord Jesus Christ, the love of God and the fellowship of the Holy Spirit be with you", we are actually calling on heavenly sources! We ask for the gentle Grace of our Lord Jesus, the abiding fellowship of the Holy Spirit and the almighty love of God from which *nothing* can separate us from, to be with us. To remain with us. To accompany us. To encircle us. To cover us like a canopy.

I held on to my son's hand and imagined as we walked home together, I imagined the angels walking in front of us, calling out "Make way, make way for the child of God." This is a picture which fills me with inner assurance and joy, and I carry it in my heart. And I thank God for my amazing child.

On the move – again

Appointments for ministers in the Methodist Church are usually for an initial period of five years. While it is possible to stay for a longer time, if both the minister and the church(es) they are serving want that to happen, the default position is that a minister will move after five years, and that applies especially when it is one's first appointment. Having begun ministry in Tottenham in 1990, I had to go through the process of 'Stationing' for a decision to be reached about where I should be serving as a minister from September 1995.

This time I could have a more active role in the decision-making, and it was agreed that I would move from Tottenham to the Sutton Park Circuit in Birmingham, where I would again have responsibility for two Inner City Churches. One of the churches was a Local Ecumenical Partnership (LEP) with the Methodist Church and the United Reformed Church working together as a single congregation. The welcome service was arranged as usual (no Trevor Huddleston this time!) and I felt reassured that I would be working with good colleagues in ministry and that the Superintendent was caring and sensitive as well as very competent as a leader and administrator.

Almost all the members in the church that was simply Methodist were of African-Caribbean origin. They were a close-knit, caring group and we got on well from the outset; they reminded me of the congregation in Notting Hill, even though the church was not as large, or as culturally diverse.

The dominant group in the LEP were English born and bred. They were dominant not only in their number, but in their control of the church; they held all the key positions of responsibility, and had developed a culture that was designed to make sure that no transient minister would be allowed to do anything that they did not approve of! We did not get on well

– right from the start. Relationships deteriorated to the point where members of the congregation would deliberately turn away and whisper to one another when I began preaching; they made clear that they didn't want to hear my sermons. I don't know why they kept coming to church.

My solace was in working in the community, being alongside people, women in particular, who did not see themselves as religious, but who knew how to look out for one another, and to help one another when things got tough. Many of these young women were single mums and lived on this vast housing estate adjacent to the church. When I tried to allow these women to have space in the church for their informal meetings with me, the leaders made it clear that they did not approve, and made things difficult for us. The situation got so bad that the Moderator for that Region of the URC was asked to come to a meeting and to be a mediator between me and the leaders.

Steps for improving the relationships were recommended, but they were not real solutions. Being a minister 'for all' was turning out to be more difficult for me than I had ever before found it to be. It was decided that though I would remain minister of the congregation, some of the responsibilities of the minister would be dealt with by the URC minister at a near-by church. It was quite revealing, I think, that when the time did come for me to leave that church, the group that expressed most sincerely their regret at my leaving, were the non-church going women I had worked with in the community; they took me on a night-out that I will never forget!

Again, I acknowledge that I must take some responsibility for the breakdown in relationship. I was not in a good place emotionally when I began the appointment; I felt isolated from all that was happening in the new South Africa; I still hoped and longed for a reconciliation with Mark. I was living in limbo. It was a period of my ministry that was for the most part OK, rather than engaging or stimulating, though there were occasional special moments and events. I became increasingly restless, and decided that I should curtail my appointment and 'return home' to South Africa.

My testimony before ordination

Before Methodist ministers are ordained in Conference and with the laying on of hands, we must give account of our calling. God is the stronghold of my life and it is important for me to testify and acknowledged how God has changed my life. This is my testimony before ordination.

"It is true that God calls us all in different ways. When I first thought I heard God calling me into His church it was not out of pure and Godly thoughts – it was initially out of pure vanity and selfish reasons. I am the eldest of five brothers and five beautiful sisters. I was made very conscious of the fact that I was not in the conventional sense "a pretty girl". In fact, one of my aunts made it clear that I was too ugly "to get a man" – so I decided to become a nun. Not that nuns are ugly, mind you! But I reckon by becoming a member of a religious order, no-one will feel sorry for me if I do not get married. As a nun my life will be given over to Christ and so it will be accepted that I can't give myself to a mere man. Our local Minister at the time, listened patiently and seriously to my tearful story and then told me to join our local Methodist Youth Club. He also told me that within the Methodist structures we do not have anything remotely similar to the Catholic Order that is for women only. Should I still be of the same mind in a year or two (I was going on 17years old at the time), he would gladly support my offer to candidate for the Diaconal Order in the Methodist Church which in those days were for women only. And in 1976 I did candidate training for the Diaconal Order. I did not complete my training.

I was brought up in a Christian home where God was spoken to and spoken about on a daily basis. My fathers' job, our daily needs, our monthly wages was offered to God. God was never in question and going to Church was as normal as breathing. I suppose in one way I grew into my calling. I was the circuit Youth Leader for several years, taught in the Sunday School and at one stage became Sunday School Superintendent in charge of the Junior section, and held other leadership positions in Church.

I believe I had three conversion experiences:

The first time was this unbelievably, crazy, supernatural experience that happened when I, and two of my younger sisters, were attending a house prayer meeting in our neighbours' lounge. As we were all kneeling down in front of the couch, eyes closed, Pastor Freddie encouraged us to ask God into our lives; to confess our sins and ask for forgiveness and ask God to make us new persons. I had my eyes tightly closed and fervently asked God to forgive my sins and accept me as His child. As I sat there with my eyes closed, I saw a vision. I really honestly saw steps going up to heaven, and at the top of the steps there was a bright light shining. Like a huge sun. And then out of this bright light a voice came. Calling my name: Jennifer, Jennifer … I was shaking and began to cry … I opened my eyes, and looked around, the others were still praying. Oblivious to my fear and awe and confusion. I don't know how I got out of that house, but I ran across the road, home – and grabbed my mother round the waist. She was standing at the kitchen sink I remember. I held on to her tightly and wept. I tried to explain to her through the sobbing what I've experienced, but I guess she was like me, out of her depth. But she held me gently and said perhaps it was the Lord speaking to me and that I should go sit quietly on my bed and wait. Wait for who or what I didn't know. But nothing happened, except that I was filled with fear. Although this memory lost its terror over the years, I still remember it clearly.

My second conversion happened when an altar call was made in our church following a Billy Graham Convention in Cape Town. I went forward full of remorse for my sins and more out of fear of going to hell. I was brought up with hell, damnation and fire if I should ever paint my nails red, or wear lipstick or have sex before marriage I shall burn in hell and the devil will poke me with his fork until I die in the fires of hell. It was sheer terror that brought me on my knees at the altar.

My third conversion experience happened years later when I found myself in an impossible situation of pain, anger and confusion; I fell in love with a man who was the "wrong colour" for me to love. Our love was declared a crime in South Africa because the Law said that love between two white people was moral and legal. But love between a white person and a person of another colour was illegal and immoral – constituted in an Act called the Immorality Act. LOVE was given a colour by the South African government. During this period of my life, God was the ONE who heard my cries of pain and my outcry of anger. During this period too, my antagonism towards white people was challenged by Mark the young white man I gave my heart to. I think that he loved away my bitterness against Whites as he slowly taught me to see the person and not the colour. Gradually my attitude started to change towards some Whites. And in this searching, questioning, floundering time in my life, I grew into a closer and personal relationship with God. I call this my third conversion, not religious, but spiritual real, and life transforming.

I have always known that God is with me. I have known God's presence in a prison cell, and at different times in my life and I know my love for God whom I cannot see, must be seen somehow in doing loving acts of kindness to those who have nothing or less than I have, so that they too, can have the fullness of life that Jesus offers to us all. To have "fulness of life", for me means that you must have enough food to eat, to have a place to call home, to be able to go where you want to without restrictions, and to love whom your heart loves. Life in this country is not easy for Mark and myself, and we face challenges on a daily basis, but the knowledge that our love for one another is sincere and that our need to be together is right, fills me with courage and the will to go on. The birth of our son Themba whose name means HOPE, continues to give deeper meaning to our togetherness. I continue to experience this tension between knowing a loving God and also experiencing pain and suffering in the world. I am the one who always ask the questions that have no answers and I know that I will continue to have conversion experiences as every day I have to learn from God how to live authentically for Him. Our personal future looks uncertain as we wait for the Home Office to make a decision about our status in this country. It has been a long road both in our loving of each other and in my faith journey, but I have hope. I shall never lose hope. I believe God has called me into His ministry – and as I stand here before you – I know in my heart that I'm not the "right stuff ministers are made of" – I nevertheless offer myself for ordination in the Methodist Church – if you will have me.

I love God. I love the Church. And I love most people – sometimes. But I know that God loves me and I want to belong to Him. I have been asked to choose a hymn that accompanies my faith journey. It was not easy to select just ONE hymn, for I have many favourites. but for tonight I have chosen "Through all the changing scenes of life, in trouble and in joy. The praises of my God shall still my heart and tongue employ". Thank you kindly for listening to me. Amen".

PART THREE:

SEEKING A BETTER COUNTRY

Angry Love

Chapter 9
And now?

Having lived away from South Africa for a long time, I've become more aware of some of the ways that South Africans speak that are 'special' to them. We say, "Will you just sit there so long", when people in England would say "Would you sit there for a while", or "for the time being". But there are some South African expressions and ways of using language that do not have an equivalent in English usage; one of those is, "And now?"

"And now?" is what we South Africans will say when we've heard someone sound off and get something off their chest, and when they've run out of breath, that's the time to say, "And now?" Or, when you've seen something that has taken ages to put together collapse completely in front of your eyes, you're almost sure to hear the words coming from behind you, "And now?"

I returned to South Africa towards the end of 1998, and there were many times in the following months, and even years, when it was as if I was standing with hands on my hips and saying with a sigh, "And Now?"

A Place to stay

I decided that I was making a clean break with England; I did not plan to return there. All my belongings were packed and shipped to South Africa; all the goods and memories that I had accumulated during my stay of nineteen years in "the Queen's Country" – from furniture and kitchen utensils to my son's train set; from photographs and cuttings of some of the many events I had taken part in, to my cherished volumes of theology and Biblical Studies. I even asked the Church's Pension Fund Trustee to pay me as a lump sum the proportion of my final pension that I would be entitled to draw. I burned my bridges as I left.

Before leaving Britain, I had made arrangements with Mark for him to rent a place where we could all stay when Themba and I arrived in South Africa. That was not ideal, but I had no other options at that time. Themba was three months away from his fifteenth birthday when we left Britain, and for him the move was a big disruption. I felt that the first thing I had to do was to find a good school where he would be able to complete his high school education. I was really pleased when he was accepted at a school that had a good reputation, it had previously been a school 'For Whites Only', and at that stage there was only a small minority of students from other ethnic groups attending.

My heart went out to my son because I could see that he was unsettled for a long time. He missed the friends he'd left behind in England, and at first he was seen as a novelty in his new school. The other students referred to him as "the English boy with the strange accent." Themba was an introvert, and being the centre of attention made him feel very uncomfortable. He was also in the minority. In the school he'd attended in England, he had been part of an ethnically diverse body, with students from China, Ghana, India and Iran. To find himself surrounded by  a group of white boys because they were curious about his accent and of course his name – which at the time was very unusual in an environment like Bergvliet High School – called upon his inner resilience. But my son had courage, and his mother's love and prayers surrounding him. As time went by, Themba adjusted to his life in a new country, but South Africa was never home to him. His heart was in Britain. And remained so for the next fifteen years.

With housing settled, I could turn my attention to finding a way of serving the community and getting some income.

Work

I thought that getting a post in the church would be no problem at all. I'd heard 'on the grapevine', that there were several

Angry Love

churches that had not been able to have a minister appointed to look after them in 1999. However, when I went to see the District Bishop, who was responsible for the placing of ministers, he informed me that there was no church appointment for me in the Western Cape.

I was feeling vulnerable and maybe that made me suspicious: was the Bishop thinking that I was capable only of serving Coloured congregations, and had he even considered the possibility of my being with a White congregation when he said there was no vacancy for me? Was I being penalised in some way for having left South Africa during the struggle, without any thought being given to what had happened to me before I left, and what I had done for the struggle while I was in England?

I was hurt and angry and couldn't have the conversation with the Bishop that I wanted to have – about what the calling to be a Minister meant to me as a Coloured South African Woman, and the hopes I had for reconciliation in my homeland. I left the meeting feeling completely disillusioned. I'm pleased to say, though, that this bad start didn't stop me from having a cordial relationship with the Bishop later on, and that when we worked together, I found him to be caring and effective leader. But in the meantime, I was left with another of those "And now?" moments.

* * *

Disappointed and disillusioned, I was beginning to question my decision to return to 'my own kindred and country'. But I was not going to give in so easily, not after what I'd been through, and most of all, because I believed that I did have something to offer the church in the new South Africa.

* * *

It was at that point those seeds sown years earlier, during my time as a Community Development Worker, bore fruit. Keith, one of the people I had worked with then, was now responsible for the Western Cape Branch of the South Africa Council of Churches and he was clearly pleased to see me again. With his support, I applied for the post of Fieldworker for the Council of Churches in the Western Cape, an appointment that was for twelve months. It was such a relief to me when I heard that my application was successful and that I could begin work.

Keith and I were accustomed to each other's ways of working; we worked well together as we navigated our way through the new political dispensation in our country. I was busy, and doing what I do best: working in the community as a person of faith and helping others to discover and let loose their faith; I saw this as my particular contribution to the building of our fledgling democracy.

And yet, I felt like a visitor, and many mornings I woke up not sure where I was, or what I should be doing. I missed the familiarity of London; I missed the cold winter mornings, and I kept thinking, "Well, this is only one year, then I'll go back to Britain", or, "Only a few more days, then something else will come up; only one more week, then something will happen." What was supposed to happen, I don't know. I lived like someone who was in transit.

Identity

There were other ways that my unease and unsettledness came to the surface. I had to train myself mentally how to live in the new South Africa. All the apartheid signs indicating where to sit in the bus, where to walk in the subways, where to queue in the post office and banks, were no more. Everyone was walking and moving where and when and how they wanted!

For months I felt odd, like something was missing, and I walked about feeling uncomfortable within myself. Whenever I saw a white woman laughing and chatting with a Coloured woman, I felt myself going tense and feeling upset (I cannot articulate what I was upset about), but my mind was searching for honesty, for genuineness: I asked myself if what I was seeing was real; whether there could be, in South Africa, real sisterhood between white and those who are not white? Was I now being the mirror image of what I had lived with for the first thirty years of my life? How should I begin to see white women in post-apartheid South Africa? Why can I not see them in the same way that I see my white female friends in Britain – as genuine friends, as kind neighbours, as women on a journey? How could I begin to unlearn, and accept without prejudice? How could I let go of the history that every white face in South Africa represents to me?

In the meantime, Themba was going through his own struggles of trying to make sense of it all; where and how he 'fitted in' within the new South Africa. As the child of a white father and a coloured mother, who was born and lived in another country with a culture so different from the one he was now encountering, there were so many levels and layers of identity for him to resolve. And all around him were people who were themselves on a road to explore who and what they now ought to become.

I knew Themba was unhappy. I could see it; and all I could do was hold him and encourage him to 'give it a try'. He spent a lot of time with my sisters and brothers and their children. Right from the start, he was warmly welcomed into 'the bosom of the family'. His cousins found him a bit eccentric because of his Englishness, his accent, and his unusual (for them) hobbies of stamp collecting and visiting old Churches. There was also his preference for drinking Earl Grey tea, rather than the red bush tea, which is a favourite across the generations in the family. However, very quickly they grew into a cousin bond of love and mutual respect for one another. To cement this bond even further, was the fact that he enjoyed going to the family Church, he was confirmed there and later went on youth camps with the ecumenical youth movement of which our church was a part.

But in spite of all the warmth, love and acceptance in the family, Themba was always looking forward to the day when we would return to Britain and he could be 'home again'. Knowing this added to my own state of unsettledness and sense of not belonging.

In my role as Fieldworker with the Western Province Council of Churches, I wandered around thinking, here we are, women and men, comrades and non-comrades, black, white, Chinese, Coloured, Muslim, Christian, Jewish, atheist, poor, rich, middle class, employed, unemployed – all of us trying to liberate ourselves into a new democracy. How did Jesus keep together such a diverse group of disciples and send them out together to be good news to the world, I asked?

As I walked familiar roads and entered familiar shops, I couldn't help also wondering who among this crowd had been active comrades during the struggle, and who had, perhaps, been informers? Who were the ones who had to flee into exile, and who had been able to remain? It was impossible to tell. And did it matter? Is my role not unchanged whatever the circumstances? My calling is still, surely, to bring good news to the poor, give food to the hungry, and to continue to break down structures so that the oppressed can be freed, especially now that the legal walls of illegal partition had fallen down?

I reflected again on the Gospel stories, and how Jesus derived his viewpoint of the world, not from the government or the power structures of the day, but from the crowds he fed, from the widow and the fishermen and from those on the edge of society, those with no status, very little money and who earnestly wanted healing. I believe that it was the Spirit who showed me that I had to start right where I left off twenty years ago, among the poor and those on the margins; to befriend those who hunger for justice, to seek out those who want more than just the removal of apartheid signs and laws. Working for the Council of Churches gave me the opportunity I needed to establish myself in the Community to build up trust and reciprocal working relationships.

A Flashback

They say your past catches up with you. During my first year back home, I was invited to a friend's fiftieth birthday celebrations. Valerina (the birthday girl), Bridget, Beattie, Sarah and I grew up together: we went from Primary School to High School together; all of us were active in the Girl Guides Movement. We socialised and introduced boyfriends to one another, and shared secrets and dreams as best friends have done through the ages. Even with a separation of twenty plus years, our friendship never wavered.

And so, not surprisingly, on my return to South Africa we picked up where we left off and I found myself in 1999 in a large hall in a setting that could have been part of a scene from a 'Bollywood' movie. A sea of colourful bodies heaving and moving around the room, everyone talking at once and nobody really listening to anybody, loud music blaring from the DJ's table and those who were not jostling to get to the food first, were having a jolly time on the dance floor.

I was part of the queue snaking round the room towards the area where scrumptious food was displayed in buffet style, but with one section where hot curry was being served by waitresses in chefs' hats.

The queue was long and this gave me plenty of time to enjoy the carnival scene in front of me. It seems that I was not the only one just enjoying the spectacle, because from behind me came a man's voice, speaking quietly near my shoulder, "I wish I could be that uninhibited on the dance floor." I turned around to face him and laughingly said that I was thoroughly enjoying the dancing and relished the thought of dancing the night away! He looked like a man in his late sixties, or early seventies, and spoke with a slight accent I could not recognise.

Well, we carried on chatting, about parties in general, about the jolly crowd in the hall, and then he said his wife did not accompany him tonight because her brother had arrived from Norway that morning. It turned out that he left South Africa in his twenties, went to Norway to study engineering, met a young lady there, fell in love and got married. He had returned to South Africa, accompanied by his Norwegian wife and two daughters, for the funeral of his mother.

We exchanged names, his was Pinda Kuzwayo, and, being my mother's daughter, I asked him if he was related to an old friend of mine, also called Pinda K. I said that many years ago in my late twenties, I used to know Pinda who was a friend of my husband Mark, at the time. And how extraordinary it was that he shared a similar name and surname! My new found friend wasn't smiling anymore; he stared hard at me. His eyes roamed my face, looked away at the party crowd and came to rest back on my face. "Whoaa, wait a minute, wait a minute... tell me again your name, it's Jenni, isn't it... Jenni, Jenni; did you perhaps work for CUPC in the seventies?" We both got rather excited and having reached the buffet table by then, piled our plates and moved away from the chatter and the loud music. Once we'd found seats outside on the patio, Pinda retold a story that was all too familiar to me since it was my story too – the story of the sealed box that I related in an earlier chapter!

Pinda was one of the two young men and to meet in this way was sheer joy. We were just so excited to meet in such an extraordinary way; and he asked me about the box. I said it must still be in the church where I hid it all those years ago. So, the week following the party, he accompanied me to the church and we told the story to the minister there, who listened with shock and amazement. He was so overwhelmed by the story that he almost ran across to the church, so excited, and shivering with anticipation; he'd brought with him a hammer and tools to remove the floor boards under the pulpit. Lo and behold the box was still there – all of twenty-three years later!

Just as before, I dared not ask what was in the box. I guess deep down I knew, but I was scared and I did not want to know. The minister's curiosity got the better of him and he opened the box. There before us lay two new and shiny firearms, guns, weapons that had the potential to kill! And I, a follower of Jesus, had been party to this. I felt sick in the pit of my stomach.

The minister, in his kindness, took the weapons and handed them in to the nearest police station where he had to make a sworn statement that they did not belong to him. He told the officer at the desk that the box was discovered under the floorboards when the Church Council took the decision to move the pulpit. He said the builders brought the box to the Manse and now he was bringing it to a safe place, the police station, because he, as a minister who had very recently arrived at the church, had no knowledge of how it came to be there. After answering some more questions, and filling in the necessary papers, this Good Samaritan reported to myself and Pinda that all was well. Case closed. I said a silent prayer asking for forgiveness for my foolish ways.

It made me realise again that the life of a minister is never dull; but I was glad that there were no further surprises like that! My first year 'back home' flew by, and soon it was time to welcome in the New Year, and our six years of democracy.

New Ministry

In the year 2000 I was appointed the Presbyter for Athlone Methodist Church and right from the beginning, I was caught up in the business of making church a welcoming place for all. I went down the familiar road of preaching, baptising infants, and marrying those who wanted the blessing of the church on their union as husband and wife. I was drawn into the incredible privilege of pastoral care among the poor, the lonely and the confused.

I remember doing an increasing number of funerals in the first half of the year, and one of the funerals stood out above many others because it was so completely different from all the rest; it was quite bizarre!

The person being buried was a member of the gang called "The Americans", which operated in Manenberg, an area near the Church. I was leading the procession of mourners into the cemetery and as we approached the open grave edged with artificial grass, I found myself welcomed by a guard of honour formed of gang members wearing balaclavas, who stood in two lines, holding aloft AK47's to create an arch for me to walk through! I didn't even have time to think, "And now?" I walked towards the head of the grave and pretended that the presence of twenty hooded men with guns is a normal part of a funeral service! I was trembling and I was afraid for what might happen if there should be an altercation between mourners and the gang members.

Only by God's grace was I able to carry through to the singing of the last hymn, after which I said the final blessing, and just as that ended, the 'guards' started firing their guns into the air as a final salute to their fallen comrade. The noise was deafening! Family and friends, and curious onlookers scattered in all directions. I lifted up my cassock with one hand and made to follow them, when a heavy hand fell on my arm and encircled my wrist in an iron grip. I heard a voice saying in very normal tones, "Just walk slowly with me out of the gates and nothing will happen to you. I promise you this." So, I was escorted away from the grave by my unknown guardian, and the rest of the gang, holding their guns straight up in the air, followed behind us and we walked sedately in relative silence, through the cemetery gates. My balaclava covered companion escorted me to where my car was parked the car, waited until I managed to start it (at the second attempt, because of my trembling hands) and gave me a regal salute as I drove away in as normal a way as I could manage!

Athlone Methodist Church was a large congregation with a missionary zeal, and they demanded and gave in equal measure. Church Council Meetings, meetings of different organisations, numerous requests for baptisms, never ending pastoral demands, Sunday service preparations, preaching, teaching catechism – the normal round of ministerial duty, took up most of my time and energy.

* * *

But I managed to make the time for reconnecting with loyal friends from my past and we got unbridled pleasure in one another's company. As we renewed the old bonds of friendship and reminisced about our shared youth, I was aware that my friends were excited about the social change happening around them and the ways in which conventions had been overthrown. The majority of my friends expressed joy and relief, and were excited about the way things have changed in South Africa. They welcomed our new dispensation. They tell me that South Africa is going in the right direction. Many supported and voted for our new ANC government and applauded its social reforms. But they gave scant attention to economic inequality, unfair labour practices, and the damaging new Apartheid that 'affirmative action' was creating. On the rare occasions when I find myself saying something even remotely 'political' I was asked in a jovial tone not to be so serious, and to just enjoy the pleasures of the new South Africa.

In our jolly little circle one day, someone remarked, "We Coloureds have gained nothing by getting our freedom from apartheid, leave the Blacks to sort out their own mess." These words, spoken in jest, left me wondering what happened to the respectful, socially conscious people I knew before I left. Again, I found myself pulled between knowing that I must do the right thing, and not having, yet, found the right time and the right place to do it. What I knew then, and continue to know, is that there is unfinished business between the different ethnic groups in the land that I love.

* * *

One never knows what each new day will throw at you, but through it all, Grace abounds as reflected in my life *then* and *now*. This sense of being wrapped in Grace, has been repeated many times over, but most poignantly when in 2003, I was privileged to attend the memorial service for the Rev. Theo Kotze, who had an immense influence in my life.

Theo was a man of God, a person with integrity who stood by his convictions of truth and justice. He was the Head of the Cape Town branch of the Christian Institute when I met him in 1974. A woman known only as auntie Florrie introduced me and I was warmly enveloped in a big bear hug by Theo Kotze. I was in a state of shock afterwards, because it was

With Rev (Dr) Theo Kotze and his wife Helen. As Methodist pastor in Cape Town Theo played a major role in the struggle against Apartheid. With Beyers Naudé he was co-founder of the Christian Institute. He was eventually banned and had to live in exile.

the very first time that a white man put his arms around me all those years ago. I met his wife Helen and their young son Stephen who I remember dropped me and auntie Florrie off at our respective homes. I was one of many young people black and white who frequented the Kotze's home in Sea Point. It was through Theo that I befriended and became a member of the Black People's Convention, whose meetings were held on the premises of the Christian Institute. In those days I had also been granted a room in the Sea Point Methodist Church to have literacy classes where I taught a small group of domestic workers.

Theo Kotze's memorial service in 2003 was one of the most moving and at the same time most celebratory, as one speaker after the other speaker shared memories of their inspirational encounters with one of Methodism's great sons and a peace maker of South Africa. '*Hamba Kahle*' dear friend and comrade, knowing you has made me a better person.

* * *

My restlessness and my feelings of not having a place where I really belonged did not get better as the years passed. I had accepted, eventually, that my marriage with Mark had broken down 'irretrievably' and petitioned for divorce, which was granted in 2000. The break-up of our marriage had a devastating effect on me, but Mark was not the villain in this break-up. For me he continues to be one of the most dedicated and uncorrupted comrades in present day South Africa. He is also the father of our son. And to me, someone who has added depth to my growth as a person. We remained in contact, not just because of our love for Themba, but because having been through so much together, it was impossible to simply cut all ties completely.

I relished being near to my family, being able to see my sisters, and my mother almost every day, and my brothers very regularly at family get-togethers of one kind or another. I enjoyed the colleagueship of the Ministers I worked with in the Dumisani Circuit, and developed good relationships with Ministers in different parts of the Cape of Good Hope District. I worked hard and, over time, introduced a number of changes in the church and in the community at Athlone, and saw the congregation grow. But in spite of all that, I did not feel that I was 'at home'. I had expected so much of the new South Africa and somehow the reality did not match the dream.

I began to think about returning to England, which, at first, seemed such a crazy idea that I wanted to dismiss it, but the thought took root, and in 2004 I found myself packing my belongings once again and getting ready for yet another new beginning, and thinking yet again, "And now?"

Chapter 10
Open to Grace

The short answer to my last "And now?" was: Shernhall Methodist Church. It's a church in the London Borough of Walthamstow, and not very far from Tottenham where I had begun my ministry as a Probationer Minister in 1990.

There were two other Ministers apart from me who were joining the Circuit in September 2004, and Rev Ermal Kirby, the Chair of the District, was the invited Preacher for the Service. He was also the first black Minister to be appointed as a Chair of District in the Methodist Church in Britain, and on the day of my welcome service, I had no idea of the significant part that he was to play in my life in the coming years.

Open doors

I had returned to England without my beloved Themba. The academic year in England starts in September, so does the Church's calendar year. Themba was in the midst of his college studies and as we were discussing my return to England, he felt that he wanted to complete his studies before joining me. It was decided that I would begin my appointment in Shern Hall Church in September, he will come visit me in December; will return to Cape Town in February to continue his studies, but will spend all his vacations with me during his three-year study course. I made arrangements for Themba to live with Jakes (my brother) and his wife Jean and their two daughters, who adored their cousin and they got on like a house on fire. On the surface he looked happy, and I pretended to be happy leaving my son behind while I begin my new Circuit appointment on my own. But I was not looking forward to it. For the very first time in my ministry, I shall be completely on my own without kith or kin! When Mark left, it was me and Themba against the world. We were a unit. He was flesh of my flesh, blood of my blood. My son, who gave meaning to my life, and whom the Lord used to help me become whole. I love Themba above anyone else on earth, and his wellbeing is my responsibility as his mother! I worried about him, but held onto the consoling factor that he was with family, that he will have a bed to sleep on, that he will have something to eat every day. It was not an easy decision for me to make, no-one in the family swan off and leave their child behind! I was riddled with guilt and fear for his safety to and from College. But there was nothing to do, but for me to get on with life and believe that all shall be well. I phoned Themba every day, and every so often during the day silent petitions for my son winged their way to God.

The manse I stayed in was big and I felt very alone and lonely in it. The first two months on my own I spent a lot of time in the spacious study, my bedroom and the kitchen. Three more bedrooms lay empty, quiet with doors I kept closed. During the day there was work to do in the community and in the church. But the nights were the longest and the loneliest. It was one such night when I was so homesick and missing Themba, looking around my big empty (of another human body) house, that I recalled the words of dear Mrs Plant, whom I stayed with all those years ago when I first came to Britain. When I once asked her if she's not afraid to live in such a big house all by herself, she said to me: "Yes, after my William died, I was lonely and afraid. Night after night I would go round checking the doors and windows three times before going to bed. I would wake up in the middle of the night filled with fear that someone might be trying to break in. Then one night, as I kneel down to pray, the words just flew out of my mouth, I said: 'Lord it's no use both of us staying awake! I'm going to sleep now. And I did just that'". Remembering those words, I adopted it for myself and laughing I spoke to God that night and went to bed comforted with the assurance that God will take care of Themba on one side of the ocean, and of me on the other side.

However, I still had a huge house all to myself and being South African and coming from a large family who only ever lived in houses much too small for our large brood, I didn't feel comfortable with all this empty space. My mind kept wondering to all those people living six to a room, and those sleeping on the streets of London and Cape Town. But I think the Lord knew what he was doing and I quickly found that this unwelcome situation could be turned into a blessing. Long before I even completed that first year in my new appointment, there was a constant stream of people staying with me, for periods ranging from a single night to several months. There were friends from 'back home' who had managed to put together the price of their plane ticket for a once-in-a-lifetime visit to England, but could not afford to stay in hotels or other commercial premises; my doors were open and my heart

Angry Love

welcomed them into my home. Fellow ministers in transit who needed a 'stop-over' place; friends who asked if I could 'look after' their children who would be coming to England on a course lasting several months, and needed the assurance that they would be with someone they could trust. Members from the congregations that I served in Cape Town. The list was endless. I hadn't planned it, but in spite of my marriage having ended, I was continuing to fulfil the additional vow that I had made on my wedding day.

* * *

In turn I found doors were being opened to me. There was so much care shown towards me throughout my time at Shernhall. There was never any shortage of homes where I could go for Sunday lunch, or for a visit during the week when I get to sample delicious freshly baked cakes and scones, my biggest weakness! I developed a special bond with a group that I refer to as 'The Girls', who would meet regularly in one another's homes, share food, talk, listen to one another's favourite music tracks, and dance 'til we could dance no more – it all felt very South African, though the rest of the group were all born in different parts of the Caribbean. This group of jolly ladies reminded me of my sisters back home, and they became my soul sisters. I enjoyed myself with them and their antics soothed and filled the gap of Themba's absence.

Ministry in the church and in the community was very fulfilling. Most of the members of Shernhall (more than ninety per cent) had their places of origin either in one of the countries in and around the Caribbean (Jamaica, Barbados, St Vincent, Guyana) or in one of the countries on the continent of Africa (Ghana, Nigeria, Zimbabwe, South Africa). They were very socially aware – alert to the reality of racism and inequality; and at the same time in tune with spiritual matters and eager to learn and grow as Christians. Prayer fellowships and a regular Bible Study group became part of the programme. Of course, there were power struggles and clashes of views here as there are in every church, but I felt very much 'at home' in Shernhall, both in the church and in our community outreach.

The social life of the church grew and became a means of drawing in the spouses of members who had up 'til then not found a way of becoming part of the fellowship. The presence of a large number of children, young people, and young adults gave Shern Hall that something special, and I worked hard to encourage and support them. I have always found that music can play a vital role in building community and giving confidence (as it did on Broadwater Farm), so I gave my support and prayers for the formation of a Steel Band. Amazingly, five young women showed interest and enthusiasm and so our 'all girls steel band' was formed during my first year as the Minister at Shernhall Methodist Church. Our hymns were sung delightfully to a calypso beat and the parents in the congregation gave enthusiastic support to their drumming daughters! This small girl band went from strength to strength; they even performed in front of the Queen in the Albert Hall one year, and are still growing now, with the addition of two young boys. I was happy and enjoyed my ministry at Shern Hall.

* * *

I suppose that there were two things that would have made me feel that my joy was complete at that time, to have Themba with me, or to be in a relationship where I could again experience the joy of mutual giving and receiving. Although I was kept pretty busy with work in the Church, I was lonely, and I was yearning for a love that was not reciprocated. My hope of the first solution was dashed when after one year, Themba told me during one of our regular phone conversations that he had changed his mind and that he was no longer planning to re-join me in England.

Moving to South Africa had been a difficult experience for him. It had taken him years to make all the adjustments that he needed to, but now he was beginning to feel that he knew who he was, and what was expected of him. He could not face the prospect of leaving all that behind once more – and, yes, there was someone there in South Africa who had become very special to him. Her name was Nicole, and he wants to be in relationship with her and I will meet her on our next SKYPE conversation.

My heart sank. I could entirely understand Themba's position, but that didn't make it any easier for me. I couldn't see any way that I could find the sense of being whole that I longed for. I felt that I was in danger of slipping back into the state of restlessness and rootlessness that I had been in before leaving South Africa for the second time. Fortunately, just in time (God's time), a way opened for me to move forward towards a more hope-filled future.

Open hearts

In the spring of 2005, I received a copied letter that Rev Ermal Kirby had sent to all the Ministers and lay members of the Synod. He shared two bits of personal information with us, which made me see, for the first time, just how open and vulnerable he was prepared to be. The first, was in relation to his health – and he used that to encourage all Ministers to take advantage of the special provision that the District had made for all Ministers to have a full medical examination at a private clinic every two years; and the second was in relation to his marriage, which he said had ended and Ermal explained that he had chosen to let the District know in this way, rather than having the news leaking out slowly.

This came as a complete shock, and when I met with other ministers in the Forest Circuit where I served, we agreed that we should let Ermal know that we were thinking of him and his family, and that we were praying for them. I felt the need to let him know, in addition, that my own experience of the breakdown of my marriage had taught me that it could be a comforting help to have someone to have a cup of coffee with, or even an ice cream – though I couldn't really see him walking through a park, licking an ice cream! He was so proper, as my mother would say. But I felt real empathy for him and wished that there was some way I could be of support. As a mere local Minister, I did not have the courage to just phone him up and say how sorry I was about the breakdown of his marriage. Although my three colleagues and I signed and send a pretty card to cheer him up, and assured him of our support.

Ermal was due to come to Shernhall a few months later, to preach at a service in which there would also be the Confirmation of a number of people that had just completed their preparation. The service would be followed by a shared lunch, open to everyone. We had to be in touch a few times to plan the service, and in one of our conversations he had suggested that perhaps he could take up my offer of going for a coffee when the service and lunch were over, and I agreed. On the day of the Confirmation, as we talked in the vestry before the service, I asked if the arrangement we made for after the service was still on, and with a perfectly straight face he responded 'Oh, yes, I've remembered our date." This response, in front of the vestry stewards who were counting the Sunday collection, took me so much by surprise, I had to quickly leave the vestry and hurry to the lady's toilet where I could let out a long breath that seemed to have been caught up somewhere in my throat.

Now, before I say any more, let me tell you a bit about the picture I had of my District Chair up to this point. To me, he was an enigma and didn't fit into any stereotypical male version I had in my mind. Firstly, there's his presence – he's tall, and handsome, and has an air of natural authority without being in any way over-bearing. And I've seen how people respond to that authority. Secondly, there's his voice – a baritone that caresses, and flows as effortlessly as soft butter spreads on warm toast. I've heard women colleagues refer to him simply as 'The Voice'. Then there's his intellect and preaching ability – he helps people see things that they were not aware of and makes connections that others miss, and does all this in a way that makes you feel that you want to draw closer to the God that this man is giving you a glimpse of.

Well, it was this paragon of virtue that I took after the service to a nearby pub for coffee, though neither of us actually had any coffee, and from there we went to an area of natural beauty not far away, where he suggested that we might take a walk around the lake. He gave me a stern look when I insisted that by South African standards this was no more than a pond. Ermal said that it looked as if it might rain, so he took his umbrella with him and held on to it like an athlete might hold onto the parallel bar with both hands for dear life, throughout the walk. (I challenged him much later in our relationship, that it was as if he needed the umbrella as his chastity belt – though I don't think there are such things for men!) For my part I just concentrated on not falling over and making a fool of myself as I tottered along on my church shoes, high heels that were totally unsuitable for an afternoon walk over uneven ground!

We found it surprisingly easy to talk with one another about a wide range of topics – spirituality, trees, South Africa, music, our families. I wasn't sure what was happening, but I was content to just let it happen, and we parted amicably enough after our time together. I hoped that in the next few weeks there might have been a follow-up, another coffee or even the long-promised ice cream, but there was no communication from Ermal, and I wasn't going to be the one making the next move.

Providence, and the Ghanaian Fellowship, brought us together again in September that year. At Shernhall there were quite a few families of Ghanaian origin. They met locally as a group quite regularly, and then once a month they would travel to Central Hall Westminster for an afternoon gathering with other Ghanaian Fellowships from around the London

District. Members of the Fellowship invited me to attend one of their meetings at Central Hall where on that Sunday, they were celebrating a particular milestone in the history of the Methodist Church in Ghana.

Ghanaian Methodists insist on showing their respect for Ministers, and they do so sometimes in ways that make me uncomfortable. When I arrived at Central Hall that afternoon, one of the members from Shernhall spotted me sitting in the congregation, and insisted that as a minister I should be sitting on the platform in the front of the church. I declined, saying that I was quite happy to stay where I was, but this dear member decided that his minister must be given due recognition, and so he grabs hold of my handbag and walked with it up the steps onto the platform. I had no choice but to follow him, or to lose my handbag – which would have been a fate worse than death for any woman of my background! I was ushered to a seat right next to the guest preacher for the service, Rev Ermal Kirby, Chairman of the District. It was the last place I wanted to be.

I tried to make the best of my uncomfortable position and relaxed gradually as the service progressed. When the time came for Ermal to preach I was able to pay attention to what he was saying. He seemed quite drained at the end of his preaching, and I reached out (as I would to any colleague in ministry), and touched his hand in a gesture of comfort and empathy.

After the service I tried to hurry away, but he asked how I was getting home and offered to give me a lift as our manses were not far from each other. I said that I would be happy to travel by public transport with the members from Shernhall, but he asked me again to let him take me home. Very reluctantly, I agreed. As we drove along, he turned to me and asked if I was hungry. I admitted that I was, a bit, as I had rushed to Central Hall after the service at Shernhall, and he said that he was too, because he had not had time to have a meal before coming to Central Hall. He suggested that we should stop at a restaurant on the way home so that we could have something to eat.

He really seemed in need of food, and so I agreed. Just a little further along the road we spotted an Indian restaurant that looked promising, went in and had a really good meal as we chatted easily with one another. As we left the restaurant, I thanked Ermal for having persuaded me to join him for a meal and, in the safety of the public pavement, reached up and gave him a kiss on the cheek in a typical South African way. He smelled nice of some kind of aftershave, and it was at that moment that I also became so conscious of him as a man. A man I felt a certain attraction for. I felt flushed and my heart was beating faster, but I walked as normal as I could to where he parked the car and he drove me to my house.

* * *

The next day was a nightmare for me! My mind wouldn't focus on anything; I kept on re-playing scenes from the previous day and wondering what was happening to me. In the end I picked up the phone, and put it down again. I did those three times before finally plucking up the courage to let it ring. I don't know if I was glad or sorry when I got an answering machine. I left a message in a voice of mock severity, asking why he had dared to interrupt the work of the Kingdom by taking my mind away from my work for the whole day. Can he call me back when convenient, please...?

My call was returned late that afternoon, and when the Chairman of District next called at my manse it was not in his role as Chair, but as the one who was bringing me healing and hope, and I found too that I was able to begin to offer him the healing love that he needed. It was a strange match and when people came to hear about it the reaction was often, 'Jenni and WHO??' Ermal was sometimes so cautious it infuriated me. Over the months we spent more and more time with each other, discovering parks and open spaces all around London that we'd never realised were there. We got to know each other better, and once, when it was his turn to come to my manse, I arranged for 'The Girls' to be there for one of the get-togethers that I regularly had with them. Ermal was surprised, and looked out of place among this group of gregarious ladies who was chattering and fluttering around like colourful birds. Swaying their hips and singing along to Bob Marley, as they filled the table with jerk chicken, roast potatoes, curried goat, and stodgy puddings. When the meal was finished, we pushed table and chairs aside and started dancing with each other, singing along at the top of our voices! It was clearly not the kind of gathering that Ermal would normally be part of, but he survived.

The year went by. My sabbatical came round in 2006: this is a time when a minister has to step aside from normal duties and responsibilities for three months, and use that time for reflection or study, or to experience something that they would not normally be able to do, and which would help them in their ministry. I decided to spend my sabbatical in South

Africa, including a period of silence at a retreat centre in Constantia, run by nuns. It was so good to be near to Themba and my family again for those months, but for some reason, I also missed England!

Ermal and I got married in June 2007, on the arm of my darling beloved son, I walked down the aisle of the historic and world-famous Wesley's Chapel. The service being led by Brian Goss, who had been my first Superintendent, and by Leslie Griffiths, Baron Griffiths of Burry Port, who was the Superintendent Minister of Wesley's Chapel, and an active member of the House of Lords. He described the event as Methodism's equivalent of a royal wedding. It was an amazing occasion, with several hundred people attending the service. The courtyard at Wesley's Chapel looked like the gathering of the United Nations, there were the South Africans some dressed in the colours of the ANC, Ghanaians in colourful traditional dress, the English in pretty floral wearing 'going to Ascot' hats, Asian congregants in sari's and my amazing all girl steel band (who had our guests tapping and dancing around the stony gaze of John Wesley's statute), in their red and black outfits looked stunning. The mood was festive and happy, and the cherry on top was the presence of my dear mother, sister-in-law Jean, and two of my best friends from home to share this momentous day with me.

Afterwards we went across the City to Central Hall, Westminster, where the wedding reception for our one hundred invited guests took place. There were two triumphs for me that day: I got Ermal to wear a pink shirt and I taught our guests to dance the Bart – a popular line dance from South Africa. I was happy that day with my new husband, my son at my side, my mother (looking every inch the mother of the bride in her green, gold outfit with matching hat) and my sister-law Jean, who read emotional goodwill messages from my absent siblings. My heart was full and happy.

Ah yes, once again GRACE stepped in to mend my heart in the form of this kind, charming and handsome man who became my husband that day! My Ermal. A serious looking man, but ah such fun to be with! Life is not easy living with someone who wears an invisible halo, but my life is so much richer and so much more fulfilling. This part of my journey is filled with self-discovery and the slow healing of all the bruised places inside of me. I have not only found love and intimacy in my marriage, but also friendship and laughter. God sent into my life a man of strength and of integrity. A man who teaches me that theology and science are partners; a man who opens up my eyes to "a world out there" waiting to be explored. A man whom I love and respect. Ermal makes me feel safe. I feel cared for and it brings contentment. I echo the words of Thomas a Kempis:

> "Love alone makes heavy burdens light, and bears in equal balance,
> things pleasing and displeasing. Love makes bitter things tasteful and sweet."

Open Minds

For many ministers the line of their ministry takes a fairly predictable path from one appointment to another until they become 'supernumerary'. There was never any chance of my ministry being like that. I think that it's good to be open to new possibilities, and that God can sometimes throw something unexpected into the pot.

The year after I married Ermal, I moved from Shernhall to become the Superintendent of the Streatham Circuit, just south of Brixton. That made us begin to think about what our future in ministry might look like. Ermal was part-way through his appointment as Lead Chair of the London District which had been formed in 2006, and he had been Chair of the London North-East District for eight years before that. He was wondering about going back to the role of an ordinary minister after his years in senior leadership, as a College Tutor, and staff member of an ecumenical body, but it wasn't clear how that could happen.

It was around then that we had a meal with the Reverend Ivan Abrahams, who was at that time the Presiding Bishop of the Methodist Church of Southern Africa. I have known Ivan since he was but a young man from my home Church, in Retreat when I was the youth leader there. Ivan talked about some of the challenges that he saw that the MCSA still had to resolve, including how to become a church that reflected both the unity and the diversity that was required in the New South Africa. He opened up the possibility of me and Ermal being able to be part of that in some way.

It didn't seem to make sense to even look at something like this: I had been in Streatham for only a short time; ministry in South Africa would be a completely different world for Ermal, when he was so rooted and comfortable in the setting in England; what would that mean for our retirement, which was not very far away? We did nothing about it for more than a year.

I threw myself into the work at Streatham. Getting to know the churches that I was responsible for, and supporting the Probationer Minister who was my colleague in ministry. Ermal gave notice that he would not be seeking an additional term as Chair of District in London and began to look at other options. In spring 2011, there was an offer that seemed perfect for him: to be part-time in a strategic academic role, and to serve part-time as a Circuit Minister.

We thought and prayed about it and were ready to accept. But then there was a delay in the appointing process, and during that delay there came an email, asking if Ermal could come to South Africa to take up an appointment that had just become available and needed to be filled; the email was clearly triggered by the conversation we had with Ivan Abraham a year previously. Long story, short, by the end of the year Ermal was moving into a manse in South Africa, where I was able to be with him for a few weeks before returning to England to wind up my ministry in Streatham and then join him 'permanently' in South Africa from the middle of 2012.

It's just as well that we'd kept an open mind, because we were going to need it to find our way through the years that followed. That, and the assurance that God was with us, was our comfort and our confidence.

Open Borders

I've struggled for a long time with the question, 'Where is home?' When I first came to England, I was clear that this wasn't home; I was an alien; I was just passing through. I couldn't wait to get back home. Then after ten years I began to feel 'at home' here, and the South Africa I had left, with all its love and anger began to seem like a different world, even though I still talked about it as home.

The shock came when I went back to South Africa for visits and heard myself saying that in a few days or weeks I would be going back home, meaning back to England! As I was getting ready to go back to South Africa in 1998, the question became even sharper. When I said to my Superintendent that I would be going back home, he asked me, "Jenni, will you be going back home, or will you be going back to South Africa?" It was an important question and I've spent a long time thinking about it and what is my honest answer. So, when Ermal and I decided that we would move to South Africa, that seemed to settle the matter, from then on South Africa would be our home.

That worked well. We knew where we were and where we could be even when we retired, and that was reassuring. There was just a slight problem in the first year, when I had to serve in Stellenbosch, which was about an hour's drive from Cape Town, and we had to split our lives between two manses. But when we went to the District Bishop and explained the problems that this was causing, he was very understanding and we found a way of us being able to live in the same manse while serving in Circuits that were much closer together.

The churches I was ministering in were very different and I could use different parts of my experience and different approaches to ministry in each one. It was fruitful and fulfilling. Ermal didn't find it at all hard to adapt to being a minister in South Africa. In Plumstead Methodist Church, the main church that he was responsible for, the majority of the members were white South Africans, and the second largest group were Coloureds; there were very few black members or attenders. Being black, but not South African, put Ermal in a unique position, and he developed good relationships in the church and the wider community.

The manse we lived in was really big and also had a big back yard. It was ideal for family gatherings. Most of my family lived within two or three miles of us, and sisters and brothers, and their children and grandchildren were in and out of the house regularly. I loved it. Its space just invited frequent socialising: there were family barbeques, and birthday parties for my sisters' children, and all my friends came from far and near to brunch, to drink coffee or have leisurely breakfast on the big *stoep*. I enjoyed living there in Palatine Road, but it never felt completely like 'HOME'.

Our nearest neighbours were friendly, and when we arrived the white Jewish man next door brought over a cake and we had a very pleasant conversation. Our opposite neighbours had six children who rode their bikes and played on the paved area in front of their house. Their young mother and I would chat over the fence and wave to each other if we happened to come out of front doors at the same time. We didn't have the kind of relationship where we could just 'drop in' to one another's homes, but there was acceptance.

Living in Plumstead gave me an insight into how the 'other third' lived. All in all, it was okay and I felt safe. How times have changed, I often thought. And how easy it is to slip into a comfortable lifestyle when you have enough money, enough food to eat, enough furniture to furnish five bedrooms, one of which was turned into a study!

There is a strict rule in the MCSA that ministers should not continue to have 'pastoral responsibility' for congregations after they had reached their sixty-fifth birthday. That time was fast approaching for both of us, and we thought that we knew exactly how we should prepare for that, making sure that we would have somewhere to live that was reasonably close to the family.

However, Ermal could see a lot of parallels between the things that he was dealing with in his ministry in South Africa and the ones he had been handling in his time as Chair of the London District. He was sure that there were connections to be made between the two places and lessons that the church in each place could learn from the other. The British Methodist Church does not have a rule saying that ministers must retire at a particular age; it's a matter of negotiation and different agreements can be reached. It would be possible, therefore, for us to spend a few more years in active ministry in Britain. That would give Ermal the chance to do the reflection and learning that he wanted to do, and after that we could still decide to settle 'permanently' (again!) in South Africa, if that seemed right at that time.

The Methodist Church in Britain has more appointments to fill each year than it has ministers available to take up appointments – that has been the position for more than a decade. It was not hard, then, for Ermal to find an appointment back in Britain. In the conversations before the final decision was taken, he had made it clear that he would be asking to be released half-time from Circuit duties, so that he could do his reflecting and exploring from an academic base – but that I would be available to cover the half of his time that was not being spent in Circuit. It was a clear win-win, and the arrangement was sealed.

What we have learned is that we don't have to live with a continuing feeling of 'not belonging' or of home being somewhere else, we have the privilege of belonging fully to (at least) two different places at the same time, England and South Africa; we are not bound by borders, and can relish the richness and diversity of being Kingdom people, people open to being transformed by Grace.

We belong to a country called God's Kingdom...

Chapter 11
Connecting

As a child I used to like lying on my back and looking up at the stars at night. Sometimes I would try to count them, but there were so many, and the more I counted, the more seemed to appear, so I gave up. Later on, I learned that one way of making sense of the stars, was to focus on some of the brightest ones and then to find other bright ones that you could connect to, and that was how we could begin to see different shapes, like the Great Bear, or the Plough.

It feels sometimes that my life has been one long process of joining up the dots, or, if you like, the stars, of my experience. I keep reaching beyond the familiar shapes that others are happy to focus on, because I see other dots, other stars, that I'm sure should be brought into the pattern in some way. In the end, it's all connected, isn't it; and our task, given by God, is to make those connections seen. And each of us can begin where we are.

Connecting families

I come from a large family, six girls and five boys, born over a span of seventeen years. We are very different and we are family. I feel blessed that I have the kind of relationship with my sisters especially, where we can be open with one another and all feel free to visit one another, without waiting to be invited, or phoning ahead to make sure that it's OK. Our children all know one another, and are part of the gathering when there is a family event – which, in a family as big as ours, is often. These cousins have started meeting together for their own gatherings, separate from the 'Aunties', and it's great to see the sense of 'family' being kept alive.

Amazingly, Ermal is also one of eleven children, though in his case it's six boys and five girls – we balance each other in family composition as much as we do in other areas of our lives! The customs are quite different in Ermal's family: they clearly love each other deeply, but if they happen to have two family get-togethers in a space of six months then someone is sure to comment, "Aren't we beginning to meet a bit too often?" Although I find this strange, I have come to accept it as the way this family, whose origins lie in the small island of Antigua in the Caribbean, prefer to keep the family ties connected.

What has been good for me is to see the way that Ermal has been accepted into my family. My nieces and nephews don't think twice about calling him 'Uncle Ermal', and my sisters treat him (again), like just another brother. I've found, too, that Ermal's family have accepted me, and I can chat with them as easily as I would with my own sisters and brothers; our conversations sometimes cover a much wider range of topics (Ermal's siblings are all well-travelled), than they do when I'm with my family in South Africa.

All of this might sound obvious or trivial, but I have come to realise how important this way of connecting can be, and it should not be taken for granted. There are so many families that have cracks and broken relationships in them. Secrets and lies can damage connections and stop us from having strong, healthy bonds within our families, and then it's harder to have relationships beyond the family that are as strong as they could be.

The borders of the family are often not water-tight, and they don't have to be. People who are not related to us by blood can become and be seen as part of the family. I have known this at different times in my life and it has been an enriching experience. Psalm 68.6 says that "God puts the lonely into families." I ask myself if this might be one way of beginning to address the problem of homelessness and isolation? It's a risky way, I know, but I'm just putting it out there, as I ask, in the African way, "How's the family?" In the African way everyone including the animals, are part of the family.

Connecting communities

Beyond the family we all have some community that we are part of. These are people we see as 'like us', or 'one of us'. The trouble is that most of us make those boundaries so limited. We do not see the other 'stars' that could be connected in. I found, again and again, in the church that there were people who were seen as 'in' and others that were treated as 'not in'. Without me even having to think about it, I often found myself being drawn to the people who were on the fringes, and then discovered that there were gifts and graces and abilities in those people that had been unrecognised and unused, sometimes for years.

And what a joy it was when they were accepted fully as part of the one community. I wonder how well we know the people who are part of our own community.

Connections are needed not just within a group of people who share an identity and purpose, but between them and other groups that are noticeably different from them. And this, probably more than anywhere else, is where I have seen the church missing the mark, and not seeming to get the point. We tend to operate on the basis that we must make 'them' like 'us', rather than on the basis of seeing them as part of us, and recognising that God is with them and is as interested in them as God is in us! So, we are willing to do things for people (sometimes!), but much less ready to learn from them the hard lessons that God might be trying to teach us.

A simple test I suggest is to look at two things in the life of our churches: first, what message does someone get when they read the printed Notices that say what will be happening in the church over the next week or month – what proportion of those activities is for the benefit of people who are part of the church in some way, and what proportion is focused on outreach, or mission, or on serving the community? The second test is to look at the church's most recent annual accounts: in the year covered, how much money was spent on the things that are seen as necessary just to keep the church going, and what proportion on things that are of benefit to people outside the church, and, perhaps, even in another part of the world?

I remember Les Isaac, the founder of 'Street Pastors', saying years ago that he could rely on it that if there was an announcement that a well-known evangelist or worship leader would be coming to the area, then scores of people from the church would be quick to sign up for such an event and even pay to attend. On the other hand, when he made an appeal for people to go out together to help vulnerable people on the streets, then he would be lucky if there were two or three volunteers. Would that be true in your church as well, and if it is, why do you think that it's like that? Why do we not take to heart passages like Isaiah 58, where God says how fed up he is with all the services and ceremonies that go on in the Temple, and would much rather see people helping out the least and the weakest in society?

I've been humbled by the examples I have seen of people who have so little themselves, and yet find ways of showing their commitment to building community. There's a man that I know in Cape Town, who has a wife and a family to support and no regular income, but whenever they receive even a small amount of money, they make sure that the food they prepare is not just for themselves, but that it's shared with their neighbours. The times when I was privileged to join them, I was reminded of the adage, "the more, the merrier." The more people gather round to eat, the more conversation, more fun, more sharing of skills and more to give praise to God not as an individual, but as a community. A community bound together by their lack of material things yet rich in the way they look out for each other, rich in their understanding of the things that matter and rich in their openness in welcoming the stranger.

I was given the great privilege of preaching at St Martin-in-the Fields in London, in a service to celebrate the release of Nelson Mandela in 1990. The service was arranged jointly by the British Council of Churches, the African National Congress and the Anti-Apartheid Movement. In my sermon I painted a picture of communities connecting that is still a vision that I cling to. I said:

> "For most of this day I have been wondering how people at home are celebrating this remarkable and long-awaited occasion, and I know that as they say at home, "People will go all out" – as I believe God did in this story. God does nothing by halves – when there is cause for celebration, as in our scripture reading tonight, then God goes 'all out' to celebrate in style. In his book Waterbuffalo Theology, Kosuke Koyame very eloquently describes achingly beautiful, God's feast of redemption. Here is my paraphrase of what he says:

> "I visualise this parable in the Bible about a wedding feast, given by a king and the guests who were invited… When the invited guests declined his invitation, he sent his servants into the townships, into the narrow dark streets, and up and down into the Council Estates… Good and bad alike he packed the hall with them. Seen in the light of the ministry of Jesus, this parable leaves us in no doubt as to what Jesus meant; God's feast of salvation is open to all. God's feast is awesome and different. God goes 'all out' … At God's feast there is no table setting, this celebration is not orderly or tidy with soft music in the background and eloquent conversation around the table. Oh no, people around the table use their fingers, spoons, some hold chopsticks in their hands, some use knives and forks. Everyone in here is hungry, and there are platters brim-full of good food.

> Then you begin to notice there is not a dinner jacket or

party dress in sight. Women wear sari's, women are dressed in blue jeans and colourful tops, long kimonos and African print dresses with colourful head bands and beads around their ankles. The men and boys fill the hall in their work overalls, cotton shirts and shorts but every face is lit up with a wide smile! Children are chasing each other round the tables and chairs, and best of all, peals of laughter fill the air. These guests do not speak softly as good manners dictate on such an occasion! Oh, no! They shout across the room and the platters of food disappear as soon as they are put down in front of them. This motley crowd of humanity exude joy and happiness as they eat and delight in one another's company... Oh yes, I forgot to say the language we hear is not only English, but Xhosa, Zulu, Afrikaans, and Punjabi.

Since our imagination has come this far, I think we might as well imagine what they are shouting about. Dare we do it in these esteemed buildings I think I dare to suggest that just for today, they are shouting, screaming at the top of their lungs, Amandla! Viva Mandela! Praise the Lord! In short what we imagined, what we see is fellowship with God and fellowship with each other. It is what we are doing now in these gracious surroundings, and I suspect that is exactly what is happening in the streets, in the homes and in churches in South Africa at this moment. The whole people are rejoicing. And I am reminded that we are all involved with God in making things new...

Just like Nelson Mandela has walked out of prison a free man to give people a vision of a new way of living for South African people, God chose us to be the expression of His redemptive and unconditional love. In his love he gave us new eyes to see the injustices around us and new hearts that will yearn and work for justice. The release of Nelson Mandela does not mean the eradication of injustice, or freedom from exploitation; it does mean that there is new life emerging. But this new life will not be an easy one and Nelson Mandela confirms this when he said there is no easy road to freedom.

This new life brings responsibility. No-one pours new wine into old wineskins. Our people and our country are at the threshold of a whole new way of living as South Africans... But what do we find? We still have the old wineskins. A people who has been through a revolution with a sharp political consciousness, a new fervour for total liberation can surely NOT pour our new wine into the old wineskins of liberal political clichés... Jesus wants us to be TRANSFORMED by the renewal of our mind. We must all continue to build new structures of justice, mutual respect, co-operation and peace.

We rejoice in Nelson Mandela's release from jail. We thank him for the sacrifices he and others have made. We salute him as our hero and our father in the struggle. Our laughter and our tears mingle with the people at home as from across the miles we are joined together to celebrate the opening of a prison door which we pray will lead to deeper commitment and opening of more doors and hearts.

God did see your acts of solidarity with us, God did hear the cries of the people and part of His answer was expressed when Mandela walked out of those prison gates...Time for celebration! Let us continue to celebrate the release of Mandela, but let us above all celebrate our God who offers total freedom and to whom we now offer a hymn of praise..."

Connecting Spirit and Action

At the heart of what I said in 1990 and at the heart of what I still believe now, is that transformation comes when the divine Spirit empowers human effort. As the Lord said to Zerubbabel when he was faced with a job that seemed impossible, "It's not by might, nor by power, but by my spirit that this mountain is going to be moved" (Zechariah 4.6). And still today we fall into the temptation of thinking that we can bring about change by strategic planning and new ideas and methods and we forget to connect with the essential resource that makes all the difference. God, the source of all life.

There is a deep lesson for us here, I think. I've come to see that it's a dangerous mistake for the church to separate social action from spiritual empowering. They need to go hand in hand. It's not good for the church to spend so much time praising and worshipping that it never has time and energy to do the things that are needed by the community in the community. But neither is it good for the church to be so busy serving or fighting for justice that it doesn't take time to be still in the presence of God, who is in any case the one that is in charge of the mission. That's why Micah 6.8 is so important, "What God requires of us is that we do justice, love with active compassion, and walk humbly with God. That's it; the whole of it."

The Methodist Church in Notting Hill was deeply committed to action for social justice, it did a lot to address the needs of people in the community and to challenge the structures and policies that led to those injustices in housing and education and social welfare. But the church always knew that it was more than a social action group; its members and leaders made time to get away for times of retreat and reflection. In doing that they were following the example of Jesus, who when the disciples got back from their mission all excited about the great things that had happened, said to them, "Let's get away for a while, just by ourselves; we need time to be still, and there's too much activity and noise here." (Mark 6.31).

I keep on praying that the church in every place will learn and apply this lesson, and I ask for forgiveness – from God, and from the people who I have been alongside in the church – for all the times when I have not made this connection as clear as I should have.

Connecting Anger and Love

I've called this book 'Angry Love', and I quoted the opening line from John Bell's song, 'Inspired by love and anger'. In all my travels, I have not yet found a Christian who did not believe in the importance and the power of love; but I have found many who have real problems with anger. The Bible does not say that it is wrong to be angry; it just says, make sure that your anger does not cause you to do something sinful. I have walked around with a lot of anger in me, but there has always been someone or something that has helped me to do something positive, something that made me think (even after an outburst of anger), further than the immediate volatile situation.

The most powerful example is, of course, the incident that we call the Cleansing of the Temple, when Jesus overturned the tables that had been set up in outer courtyard of the temple and were being used as a 'Currency Exchange Bureau'; he then took up a whip and chased out the people and all the animals that had made it seem more like a livestock market than a place of prayer. The anger of Jesus was triggered by two things, exploitation and exclusion.

The exploitation was that people were being 'ripped off' by the money traders who were fixing the exchange rates to make sure they made as much profit as possible, or by livestock dealers who would claim that there were blemishes in the animals that poor worshippers had brought to be offered as sacrifices and then insisting that they would have to buy one of the 'guaranteed acceptable' animals or birds that the trader could sell them. The exclusion was, that while this activity that could be seen at its best (if we leave aside the exploitation for the time being) as an important and helpful preparation for worship, all of it was taking place in the Courtyard of Gentiles, the only space that allowed a non-Jew to get moderately close to the action when worship was happening in the sanctuary.

I wonder: are there examples of exploitation and exclusion around us today that could or should stir us to action? Because I believe that when we take such action, even though it cost us our lives, we show that we really are followers of the one who came to join, to connect all things and all people in himself, and gave his life in that cause. As I mull over this incident in the temple where Jesus drove out the money lenders, I believe that it was his anger against exploitation and his love for those on the receiving end that caused him to act. I ask myself where in my life does (did) love and anger meet? It's not an easy question and certainly for me, does not have a neatly pre-meditated answer at the ready. I remember when I first returned home back in 1999, I perceived a certain attitude of 'arrogance' among some young people. Especially those coming from previously disadvantaged communities. It shocked me as someone from an older generation that I perceived a lack of respect, a lack of common decency and this caused mixed feelings within me. Love and anger vied for equal place in my new found awareness. On the one hand, I am proud to observe, and to grow the younger generation who now can walk tall and free to celebrate and live their young lives to their fullest potential in a free country. I feel deep love for this generation who now takes up the baton for a non-racial and free society. And on the other hand, I feel anger at their lack of appreciation for what went before. From my perspective I want the 'born free's' to hold our recent past in mind and heart. I want with all my heart for the new South Africa to flourish, to grow in unity – and also not forget the heavy price that was paid by those who had fallen in the struggle for our present freedom. Not to forget those who were driven into exile, and those who still suffer the consequences of our recent fight against apartheid. Love and anger agonised within me as I learn on my journey, both in England and in South Africa, that anger can be a spiritual alarm bell alerting me that something is damaged, something is out of line with the will of God (as far

Angry Love

as I can understand the will of God from my limited human perspective), and the purpose of a God who is loving and just. I read somewhere that anger is a spark that can ignite action. But anger does not provide the fuel for transformative action. That comes from love. And it is this overriding love I have for my country, that motivates me to constantly ask: "how can I offer loving service and openness of heart and mind to people whose stories are different from mine?"

Angry Love

Epilogue

Singing a New Song

Looking back, I can hardly believe that it's me that's been on this journey! And at every stage of the journey, in every place that I've been, it's as if I have been asked to sing a song, and I've had to find the words and the melody that was right for the people I was with at that time and that place.

Through all my time in England I was called on repeatedly, first by the ANC and then, after the change of Government in 1994, by the staff at the South African Embassy, whenever there was an occasion where they thought that some form of 'spiritual enriching' was needed. This could be to offer an opening prayer at a meal or an event, to make a speech that would offer encouragement at a difficult time, or to give the Eulogy at a Funeral or a service of Memorial; and sometimes it was just to be present, accepted fully as part of the rich diversity that is South Africa.

It has been my privilege over the years to take part in:

- Memorial Services, where I gave a Homily, for Adelaide Tambo; Miriam Makeba; Eleanor Kasrils; May Brutus; Mlungisi Sisulu;
- The unveiling of a plaque in memory of OR Tambo, outside the House in Muswell Hill which had been the London home of the Tambos – saying a prayer of Thanksgiving for the life of Oliver Tambo, with President Jacob Zuma at my side;
- Twelve years of annual meetings of a group of which I am a founder member, South Africans at Prayer, which invites South Africans in Britain to come together once a year to focus specifically on the situation in South Africa.

In all these roles and all these places, and in others that I have not mentioned, I have seen myself as simply fulfilling my calling to serve my God and my people. And through these different occasions I have been learning a new song, a song which I gave voice to at a gathering in Coventry in 2016,

(A conference on Reconciliation), and which I share, in part, with you now:

* * *

When I shared bits of my story with a group of women in Birmingham, one of them said to me: "You must learn how to walk on the broken pieces." She said that all the little bits of my life either come from others who I have allowed into my life, or they are the pieces that I have grown, the pieces that shaped me. And I have to consider all these pieces if I want to become a whole person.

I remember her words as I look back over my life. I am a different person from the young woman who set foot on these shores almost forty years ago. I have gathered into myself other broken pieces and a new world has opened up and I have learnt to sing the Lord's song to a different tune. I sing the Lord's Song in this country – aware of Britain's imperialist past – I sing it with gratitude for the many open hearts and open doors that welcomed me. I sing it for, and with, those who have stood in solidarity with our struggle. For kindness shown to me in unexpected ways, for the generous hospitality from British families, and for my husband Ermal who is teaching me to be brave and strong and vulnerable and to not be afraid to live.

I sing a song of thanks to the South African and British Methodist Churches, who have nurtured my faith. In 2005 the British Methodist Church bestowed upon me a sacred privilege when I was elected to represent the Church on the World Methodist Council (representing over 80 million people worldwide). This position gave me the unbelievable immense opportunity of international travel for six years as a member of the Executive Committee, to different countries including Mexico, Korea, Australia, and Chile. To engage in dialogue and sharing in worship with the global Methodist family of different cultures and languages, gave me an inward glimpse of "the great multitude before the Throne".

As I recognise and embrace all the blessings I continue to receive, I listen to a gurgling inside me that begin to make up the lyrics of my new song. Like Mary, the mother of Jesus, I sing out, "The Lord has exalted his lowly servant and put a new song in her heart." ....

* * *

Angry Love

Before me I see a colourful tapestry of a rich life that was, and is mine to live. My new song is a song of Healing, Transformation and Hope – the Lord's Song – ever old and ever new. Together we, the peace makers find words to speak and sing of our common quest for justice. We sing my new song in solidarity with many voices and different accents and discover power in all the broken pieces that bind us together. I will probably never stop singing this new song because every day such precious memories of smells, flavours, and faces emerge that evoke a feast for my mind and senses. I sing about friends; Jonah from Zimbabwe, Gorge from Brazil, Catrine from Switzerland, Sharief from Pakistan, and Elsa from Bolivia, who have entered my home, sat round the table as we broke bread together. Laughter and tears as we shared not only delicious food, but the stories from our respective countries. And the Spirit of Jesus opened up my mind to see that ultimately, at the end of the day we are all just people – as they say in Cape Town, "I'm just a person." A human being with all of the frailties, hopes, fears, and dreams of every other human being. And I am reminded with such clarity of the words of Mahatma Ghandi when he wrote: "I have walked all over the world and everyone I met was my sister and my brother." One human family, one world.

* * *

I sat in conversation with a colleague from the Anglican Church who told me of an incident that happened during the request for prayer of intercession or of gratitude. An elderly congregant came forward and tearfully spoke of how the house of her employer had caught fire. She had managed to drag the woman to safety. "It is for this reason," she said as she unknotted the hankie she took from her bosom, "that I want to thank God for giving me the strength to save the life of another." She placed R50 note in the offertory plate. This is a huge amount to give away for a domestic worker, who earns pittance. Even more poignant is the fact that this is an elderly Coloured woman, who slaves away daily in the household of affluent whites, and she chose to live, not with bitterness about the past and what had been done to her, but by living in an attitude of thankfulness and grace and seeing 'the other' as just another woman who needed her help. To see one another as human beings; a person just like me.

South Africa today needs people like this woman. South Africa today needs honest people with a strong social and moral conscience. People who just want to live in harmony with others and simply seek to do good. Such random acts of kindness and reconciliation are wide spread and pour forth from ordinary South Africans daily.

Acts of generosity of heart and mind occur in the midst of homelessness and deprivation. Across the denominations, churches organise socials and worship services with the sole purpose of bringing together people who had previously been divided along racial lines.

Despite the prevailing socio-economic challenges of inequality, joblessness and poverty, the continuous racial tensions, political instability, the corruption and even lingering violence, which is often portrayed in the domestic and international media, South Africa remains remarkably resilient. Signs of hope are being erected everywhere, constructive involvement by all sectors of society is growing, as well as transformational, visionary leadership. Reconciliation is happening, often in obscure places and with life-changing consequences around the country. The churches are regaining their prophetic voice and providing moral guidance. People of all race groups are reaching out and taking hands, together building the South Africa we dreamed of, worked and prayed for: a non-racial, just, equal, humane, safe and free country for all its people, as envisaged in the South African Constitution. Young people, in my own family as well as my grand children, are busy building and living this beautiful new reality - singing a new song.

Sometimes when our own words can't express all that we want to say, we find that someone else has said it for us - and that is beauty and miracle of the Psalms and of Poetry and hymns. So, hear my new song, finally, in the words of Michael Foster:

Celebration Song

Tune: Battle Hymn (H&P 242)

1. There's a song of Celebration that is ringing round the earth,
As humanity unites to sing of dignity and worth,
Out of poverty and anger God is bringing hope to birth:
Let all creation sing!

Chorus:
Sing of hope and liberation,
Sing of justice and salvation,
Sing with holy indignation:
Let all creation sing.

2. It's a song of solidarity, of protest and of pain,
On behalf of all who suffer for another person's gain,
It's a call to faith and freedom that will never be in vain:
Let all creation sing!

Chorus:

3. It's a song that's sung in unison, but heard in harmony,
Many voices, many accents and a trillion ways to be;
And it liberates the wealthy as it sets the needy free:
Let all creation sing!

Chorus:

4. It's a song of humble penitence for all we haven't done,
It's a song of glad thanksgiving that the journey has begun;
It's the promise of a future when the world will be as one:
Let all creation sing!

Chorus:

17 December 2008

Reverend Jenni Sweet
59 Mitchum Lane
Streatham
London
SW 16 6LW

Dear Rev Sweet

I wish to express my deepest gratitude to you for directing the programme at the memorial service for Miriam Makeba held at South Africa House on Saturday, 29th November 2008.

This could have been a very sad occasion as Miriam 's passing was so recent and she was known and loved by so many at the service. Your kind words and stories helped to bring together what could have been a lengthy service. You are always graciously stepping in, often at very short notice, to assist the High Commission with our memorial services. We are eternally grateful to you for your assistance.

The service was a very fitting tribute to our Mama Africa, whose life and presence clearly touched so many lives. A true South African, African and global citizen, Mama Africa used her talent and music to fight for a better life for all.

Thank you once again on behalf of all at the High Commission, and also Miriam 's grandson, Lumumba Lee, for helping us makes this a fitting tribute to a great artist, and an occasion that will live long in our memories.
Yours sincerely

Lindiwe Mabuza
High Commissioner

South African High Commission, South African House, Trafalgar Square, London WC2N5DP
Telephone: +44 (0) 20 7451 7124 / 5   Facsimile: +44 (0)2 0 7451 7287

174   *Angry Love*

Lightning Source UK Ltd.
Milton Keynes UK
UKHW022040130422
401545UK00010B/124